IN PRAISE OF

GROW. GROW RIGHT. GROW RIGHT NOW.

"At twenty-two years old, I interviewed for a job with Jaime Hepp. From that initial moment, I knew this man was a leader, and I wanted a relationship him. I've known Jaime for twenty-plus years, and I've seen him directly and indirectly change young men and women's lives. The world needs more Jaime Hepps. Enjoy learning from Jaime's stories, experiences, and wisdom."
—**Patrick Bet-David,** founder of Valuetainment, host of PBD podcast, author of *Your Next Five Moves* and *Choose Your Enemies Wisely*

"Jaime Hepp's Grow Right principles reflect servant leadership in a wonderful way. Although he wrote down these stories for his children, everyone can relate to Jaime's 'we all can do better' theme. Read this feel-good book—then get out there and make a difference!"
—**Ken Blanchard,** coauthor of *The One Minute Manager®* and *Simple Truths of Leadership*

"Jaime's authenticity and passion leap off every page of this book, just as they do in his life. It's a testament to a life lived with unwavering commitment—giving 100 percent to everything he does. His insights on creating a fulfilling career and meaningful relationships are both inspiring and actionable. This book is a gift—a reminder that true success comes from living in alignment with your deepest values."

—**Jen Bricker-Bauer,** *New York Times* bestselling author of *Everything is Possible,* speaker, and aerialist

"In a world that never stops changing, where challenges are as abundant as opportunities, Jaime introduces us to a philosophy—a way of life—rooted in the belief that improvement is not a destination but a lifelong journey.

Throughout these pages, you will find wisdom, anecdotes, and practical advice that will empower you to take charge of your own growth. Jaime's words resonate with authenticity, borne from his own experiences, trials, and triumphs. He has walked the path of self-discovery, and now he generously shares his insights so that we too may find the strength to become the best version of ourselves.

As you turn the pages of this book, allow yourself to be inspired by Jaime's unwavering passion for growth, his genuine belief in the human capacity for change, and his boundless enthusiasm for helping others unlock their full potential.

Thank you, Jaime, for the example you have set for me in business, how you show up for your family and your community, and your belief in God. You have been an incredible example for the twenty-five-plus years I have known you. I am proud to call you my friend."

—**Vera Quinn,** CEO and president at Cydcor

"Having spent my entire life working with, working for, and working alongside the world's highest performers, I've noticed a common thread—they all choose to have a beginner's mind and they are driven by the pursuit of growing and growing right. Jaime has written a masterful playbook on how each of us can do the same to improve our performance, achievement, and most importantly, our enjoyment of life."

—**Alan Stein Jr.,** author of *Raise Your Game, Sustain Your Game*

"Having witnessed Jaime's journey for over twenty-five years, I can attest to the power of his principles. This book encapsulates the wisdom he's gained, offering a practical road map to a life well lived. His insights are not just inspiring; they're transformative. It's the kind of book I want my grandchildren to read—a legacy of values that truly matter."

—**Gary Polson,** mentor and executive chairman at Cydcor

amplify
an imprint of Amplify Publishing Group

www.amplifypublishinggroup.com

Grow. Grow Right. Grow Right Now.: Practical Wisdom for Cultivating Character and Sowing Success

The author has tried to recreate events, locales, and conversations from their memories of them. In order to maintain their anonymity in some instances, the author has changed the names of individuals and places, and may have changed some identifying characteristics and details such as physical properties, occupations, and places of residence.

Although the author and publisher have made every effort to ensure that the information in this book was correct at press time, the author and publisher do not assume and hereby disclaim any liability to any party for any loss, damage, or disruption caused by errors or omissions, whether such errors or omissions result from negligence, accident, or any other cause.

For more information, please contact:
Amplify Publishing, an imprint of Amplify Publishing Group
620 Herndon Parkway, Suite 220
Herndon, VA 20170
info@amplifypublishing.com

Library of Congress Control Number: 2024914972

CPSIA Code: PRV1124A

ISBN-13: 979-8-89138-308-1

Printed in the United States

This book is dedicated to my beautiful wife, JoAnne, and our three wonderful children—Dane, Annalise, and Vienna. Your boundless love inspires me to grow as a husband and father.

JAIMEHEPP

JAIME_HEPP

GROW.
GROW RIGHT.
GROW RIGHT NOW.

Practical Wisdom
for Cultivating Character
and Sowing Success

JAIME HEPP

amplify
an imprint of Amplify Publishing Group

Contents

Author's Note xi

Introduction 1

Thankful for Alcoholism 3

The Beauty of the Struggle 9

Who's the Best Teacher? 11

What Are the Chances? 13

Chicken Little 21

Do the Math 25

I Want It All 29

Bananas, Dry Cleaning, and Mom 35

You Don't Choose Your Values 43

Grow. Grow Right. Grow Right Now. 47

Make Today Your Masterpiece 53

Find a Mentor 61

The Impact of Self-Talk 69

Whom Are You Serving? 75
Wear Your Jersey Well 81
The Domino Phenomenon 85
The Diamond Rule 89
Willing to Experiment 95
Expect the Worst and Hope for the Best 101
Stuck behind the Pace Car 103
Mr. Learn-It-All 107
Gournal 111
Life-Changing Events 115
EGO 121
What Glasses Are You Wearing? 125
Pay Now, Play Later 131
Final Thoughts 135

Author's Note

Most of us aspire to achieve success, understanding that this journey requires growth. Yet if we accumulate wealth, advance in our careers, and climb the branches of success without maturing and nurturing our character, can we truly call ourselves successful? Imagine the disappointment of realizing that the tree we've been climbing bears no lasting fruit.

Our character must be the foundation—the rich soil that ensures our tree grows strong and true. Just as a tree needs fertile ground to thrive, our personal and professional growth must be rooted in strong moral principles.

"Growing Right" means prioritizing growth in areas that define our legacy, such as character and how we treat others. It's about ensuring our internal soil is rich and nurturing, allowing our trees to flourish, bear delicious fruit, and reach their full potential. This way, our achievements are built on a solid foundation of integrity and ethical values.

This book challenges us to ensure our trees are rooted in fertile soil as we drive our lives forward, compelling us to grow in ways that truly matter and will be remembered long after we're gone.

Introduction

In 2009, my beloved wife, JoAnne, and I were expecting our first baby. We spent many years planning and preparing for a family, and this was our moment. As our little baby boy was growing inside of JoAnne, she encouraged me to write letters to our child (and eventually multiple children). She thought it would be important in our children's development to clearly know that their parents love them unconditionally. I thought it was a great idea, and I jumped at the chance to write letters to them. Every month since that conversation, I have diligently written letters to all three of my children. I share my thoughts and feelings, and I try to capture as many great stories as possible of the experiences we share together. In each entry, I try my best to express my love and affection for each of them.

As I began writing letters to my children, I kept thinking of an episode of the Oprah Winfrey Show that left an impression on me as a teenager. Oprah had a young father as a guest on her show. His name was Dr. Randy Pausch. Dr. Pausch was diagnosed with pancreatic cancer and was given a few short months to live. He had three small children who would grow up not knowing their father. He did not show up on Oprah seeking pity; rather he was upbeat and delivered a great presentation regarding some incredible life lessons that he wanted to share and record for his children before he passed away. He was clear that his message was intended for life and how to live; it was not a message about death.

This motivated me to capture some of the wisdom that I had gained through my work, travels, and experiences if I "expire" before my children have the chance to get to know me personally. Along with a number of loving letters I wrote for my children, I also decided to write this book. I want my children to know who their father is, and I want to inspire them with stories of personal growth, discovery, and the constant quest of reinventing ourselves. I want them to feel bold and empowered knowing they have the ability to persevere through any circumstance that life presents them, and there is a good chance they'll come out on the other side as better people.

As I wrote these chapters and lessons, close family and friends encouraged me to make myself a little vulnerable and share them with a larger audience than just my children. I found so much value in the growth I experienced from great literature and coaching that I received over the years, and I hope that my stories and journey might benefit you, the reader. I hope the "Grow. Grow Right. Grow Right Now." principle or, for simplicity's sake, the "Grow Right" principle in this book can set you on a journey that will benefit you and those around you. I believe that the world desperately needs people who are motivated to be upright citizens and add value to others. These principles have the potential to drive you to become better, improve your family's environment, and make your community shine with you as a member.

I'm trusting the Grow Right principle will encourage you to embark on a constant quest of leveling up. I'd like you to develop an insatiable appetite and hunger for reinventing yourself and to never be satisfied with the status quo.

We do not have to settle. We don't have to settle for subpar careers, unhappy marriages, or stagnant, unfulfilled lives. I believe that our potential is our gift from God; what we do with that potential is our gift back to God. I hope the book inspires you to become the best version of yourself.

I wish you the best of luck on this journey.

Thankful for Alcoholism

The best place to start is at the beginning—what it was like for me as a kid growing up in Humboldt, Saskatchewan, Canada. I love the little town that I grew up in. I was fortunate to be surrounded by great people who have since become lifelong friends. However, the household that I grew up in was a little challenging. Since the time I can remember, my father was an alcoholic. Alcoholism was not uncommon in our family, nor was it unusual in our little town. Just about all my friends' fathers were heavy drinkers. Maybe it was the long, cold, dark winters that drove people to the bottle. Maybe it was considered the social norm in this little farming town. Maybe there were voids in their lives that they were trying to fill with alcohol. I'm not sure, and I'm certainly no expert on alcoholism. All that I know is that it seemed like it was everywhere around me.

My father was a schoolteacher during the week and a heavy drinker on the weekends. It was routine for him to be intoxicated every weekend and pass out on the couch. I think if he had been left alone, he probably would have left everyone else alone also. It's not like he'd drink and go around picking fights. He'd mind his own business in the garage, and for the most part, he'd get around to getting some chores done. The one picking the fights was my mother, as she had a low tolerance for my dad's drinking.

She'd wake him up from passing out and start yelling at him. The screaming would begin, and occasionally, the fights would turn physical. I was terrified as a child. There was the fear of yelling and threats, and there was the uncertainty of the future. My mother was concerned that she'd have to raise three children as a single mother on welfare. This anxiety was passed along to my siblings and me. All of us begged my father to quit drinking, and he made some sincere efforts to quit, but he eventually found his way back to alcohol. Outside the home, most people were unaware of the drinking rage. However, if the public was paying attention, there were certainly some tells that something was wrong—from a couple of DUI's to a biking accident that left an indent of his lower jaw in the pavement.

This made me a shy and insecure kid. Elementary school years were very difficult for me, even though my classmates were all very sweet children, and I made some lifelong friends in my early years. I dreaded lunchtime the most because there was no teacher to speak in front of the class—we'd all have to sit there and talk to each other. Often, I felt embarrassed and didn't say much. I watched the clock tick away, hoping I could get through lunch and begin class again. I would just hope that no one would draw attention to me—the quiet kid just trying to mind his own business. I had low self-esteem, I didn't think very highly of myself, and I was riddled with anxiety. I didn't have high expectations for my life amounting to much.

I was lucky in middle and high school. I excelled in school, and I hit a nice growth spurt in seventh grade. I was a pretty good athlete and had some good grades. I found identity with my peers and had a few great circles of friends. I was looking forward to becoming an adult, finding my way through life, and moving out of my home to get away from the alcoholism and the fighting.

I moved out of the house at nineteen years old. I expected that my parents would eventually get divorced and that my dad would drink his way to death. Unfortunately, there was a history of alcohol and tragedy in our family, and it seemed that he was destined for this ending. However, that is not how this story unfolded.

My father quit drinking at the time I moved out of the house. Of course, I was skeptical because he tried to quit drinking multiple times throughout my childhood. He joined Alcoholics Anonymous (AA) and met some great people who guided him through his recovery. Thank God for Jim and Clair. I love those two men, and I'm grateful for their love and concern for my father and for leading him through his recovery.

As my father worked on his sobriety, I focused on figuring out and advancing my career. I called and checked in with my parents weekly, curious about how he was winning this battle that I didn't expect him to win. He shared some of his learnings with me as I checked in. He developed a relationship with his "higher power" and recommended that I read *The Sermon on the Mount,* by Emmet Fox. My father's recovery and Emmet's book inspired my personal search for God and my purpose in life. My father told me that alcoholism is cunning, powerful, and baffling. When he was twenty-four, his brother died from alcoholism. My father stood over his brother's grave, vowing that he would never let alcohol take over his life like it had with someone he loved so much. Yet eighteen years later, as he entered the door of AA, he was completely baffled at how he ended up there. He taught me about the accountability and the meetings that they had in AA. As time went on, my father eventually became a DUI instructor and a sponsor for other alcoholics trying to overcome this deadly illness.

On one occasion, my father told me that he was thankful for being an alcoholic. If it weren't for his battle with alcoholism, he wouldn't be in a position to help so many people, and he wouldn't have a relationship with his higher power. Of course, he had regrets about how he ran the household and the pain he put our family through, but he came out of that entire experience with a heart of gratitude. That conversation left an unbelievable impression on me.

My dad, the man whom I once pitied, had reinvented himself (by the grace of God) and charted a new course for his life. He found more meaning in his work as a schoolteacher, his relationship with my mom improved, and he committed his time and energy to our local credit union, where he became the chair. He led Conexus to become the sixth-largest credit union in Canada, with over $7 billion in assets by the time he left. My father became an awesome role model for me. He showed me that no matter what path I find myself on, it's never too late to make the necessary changes and put myself on a better path. I was also inspired by his attitude of gratitude for the roadblocks in life, in his case, alcoholism.

With this newfound inspiration, I, too, wanted to reinvent myself. I wanted to get over my insecurities and low self-esteem. I wanted to replace my shyness with confidence and put myself on a track to building a great life for myself. If my father could come out of his darkness and find himself as a better man on the other side, then it was possible for me too. The "Grow. Grow Right. Grow Right Now." principle was born inside me.

At the age of twenty, a friend of mine told me about how much he was learning from a new book he was reading. It was written by a Southerner from Yazoo City, Mississippi—Zig Ziglar. I purchased his audio lecture *Success and the Self-Image*, and I put the cassette into my state-of-the-art ghetto blaster (that had auto-reverse) right before going to bed. I thought that maybe my subconscious would cement Zig's thoughts and wisdom as I fell asleep. I'm not sure if it did, but I certainly developed an addiction for success literature.

After Zig, I was introduced to Tony Robbins. When I was twenty-one, I spent $1,000 to attend one of his seminars. At the time I think I had a net worth of around $1,001, so you get the picture. At first I thought that all the hype and positivity around the seminar was a little hokey, but I kept an open mind. Tony started his seminar off with this: "How many of you come from a 'functional family'?" The crowd of a few hundred people was silent; no hands went up. "Okay, so now that we can all admit that we come from dysfunctional families, can we let go of our limiting beliefs and start to put our new selves together?"

That thought really caught my attention. Do we all come from dysfunctional households? Even right now as I write this, I think of the household that I'm leading. I'd like to think that I have my "stuff together" for the most part and that my kids will reflect on their childhood memories with gratitude. But it seems no matter how hard parents try or how good the intentions are, everyone will grow up in some kind of dysfunctional household.

Yes, the first step, as we Grow Right, is admitting that we are flawed.

A common question that I'm asked is, "What was your biggest challenge when you first started in business?" My answer is, "We all have the exact same challenge. Hold up that mirror in front of you and you'll see a flawed, dysfunctional human being. My challenge was me and the stories I was telling myself. Your challenge is you and the mental garbage you're carrying around. If we want to win the battle and succeed in our relationships and careers, we must take a good, honest look in that mirror. Identify and keep the qualities we, and others, admire—the good traits. But the mental garbage? We can all stand to lose that. Purge the 'stinking thinking' and replace it with a new mindset—a mindset of the new you."

That kind of response can make many people scratch their heads, but it's an honest answer. My father had the courage to look in the mirror and make the necessary changes. He conquered alcoholism and became a better man because of that difficult journey. He's a great role model to me; his example of bouncing back from despair has had the biggest impact on my life. He taught me that no matter what hand we are dealt in life, we have the opportunity to overcome all obstacles and reinvent ourselves with a better hand. The enthusiasm to reinvent ourselves is compounded when we learn not only to accept the tough things in life but also to be thankful for the tough things. That's maturity. That's powerful.

The Beauty of the Struggle

Growing up in Saskatchewan, we would see beautiful butterflies every summer. I remember learning as a kid that these butterflies come from caterpillars. I was in awe that this insect that I considered so ugly could become something so graceful and beautiful. I was intrigued, so I studied them.

As a kid, I thought in really simple terms: when the caterpillar was mature and ready, it would spin a cocoon, and it would magically transform into the butterfly. However, I learned that this process wasn't just a thing of beauty; it was a thing of struggle. If an admirer wanted to help the butterfly out of the cocoon, they would inevitably kill it—not because of bad intentions, not because of carelessly squishing vital body parts. They'd kill it because they would deny the caterpillar the importance of struggle. If they would break the cocoon for the caterpillar, it would come out of the cocoon unharmed, but it would lack the strength to carry its own weight. In other words, the butterfly wouldn't be strong enough to fly. By breaking out of the cocoon on its own, with its own strength, the butterfly would develop the necessary strength in its wings to fly. The more difficult it is to break out of the cocoon, the stronger the wings will be.

I say this because a good place to start our journey is by rethinking how we look at our struggles. Just as my father came to a place where he was thankful for being an alcoholic, we, too, can become thankful for our struggles.

I believe growth occurs when we endure through pain, when we stretch ourselves and our comfort zones. Muhammad Ali only started counting his reps during workouts once he was in pain. He didn't feel it was necessary to count the "prepain" reps because that's not where the growth came from. Growth came from multiple repetitions while enduring pain.

Growth does not happen when we are succeeding. What exactly are you learning when you're winning or succeeding? I would argue "not a lot." Success is your reward for making it out on the other side of failure. Some people call this "failing forward." You fail your way to success. Some have said that if you want to increase your rate of success, double down on your failure rate. Just hurry up and fail faster—that is how you succeed quicker. The butterflies teach us that failure and struggle are necessary ingredients for transformation. The beauty is in the struggle; the beauty happens because of the struggle. Never let a good trial go to waste. Learn from it, grow from it, pay it forward.

Who's the Best Teacher?

I have heard that experience is the best teacher. However, I'm not exactly sure that's a true statement. If it were, we'd all be geniuses by now because of how much experience we gain all the time. What turns experience into insight and wisdom are evaluation and reflection.

It's easy for us to take the short lives of caterpillars or butterflies and have the wisdom to know that their struggles are part of God's plan for these little creatures to grow from crawling insects to flying marvels of beauty. It's easy to gain insight when we are on the outside looking at something or someone in a short time frame. But in our own lives, it's difficult to have foresight and confidence when we're in the midst of the struggle. Winston Churchill gets the credit for a quote that goes something like this: "If you're going through hell, keep going." In other words, don't stop to take a selfie when things are difficult; keep moving.

There's a part of the 405 Freeway in LA that splits into nine lanes traveling southbound. As a driver, you have many options and speeds to choose from, but stopping isn't one of them—you must keep moving. This is much like life and personal growth. Just as you can't come to a halt on the freeway, inaction in life can bring our personal growth to a standstill.

When we finally emerge from the temporary struggles we face, it's essential to take time to reflect and learn from our experiences. Just as a driver might reassess their route to avoid future traffic jams, we need to evaluate our paths to avoid repeating past mistakes. Evaluated experience is the best teacher. Asking ourselves the right questions is crucial. Start with, "How did I end up in that difficult situation in the first place? How can I navigate better to avoid similar pitfalls in the future?"

By reflecting on our experiences, we can gain valuable insights and continue to grow, even while moving forward. Life, like driving on a busy freeway, requires constant motion, adjustment, and reflection to ensure we're on the right path and moving toward our goals effectively.

I enjoyed watching *The Pursuit of Happyness,* starring Will Smith. It's an inspiring movie about how a very dedicated father turned his life around. After watching it, my first thought was, "They should make a prequel to that movie. What decisions were made that put Will Smith's character on the trajectory to become a homeless father?" Of course, the real lesson of the movie is about perseverance, and it's a great underdog story. I just like the evaluation of going through hell to be noted, observed, and avoided for future use.

What Are the Chances?

In my college days at the University of Saskatchewan, an accounting professor observed that many in our class were ultrafocused on getting great grades, so he asked us to close our books so he could give us some great worldly advice. He said, "Your good grades will get you the job interviews. Your great people skills will get you the jobs." Until I heard this advice, I was under the assumption that professors were only concerned about their students acquiring the right knowledge from the classes they taught. This professor seemed to be telling us to put the books down and make sure we find ways to level up our social skills. With the help of my brother, I took on my first sales job in Edmonton, Canada, later that summer. I knew I needed to improve my communication skills. I needed to learn how to be a better listener and an effective speaker. I thought that I might want to be a lawyer one day, and I kept thinking that no one would hire me if I couldn't convince a jury, so getting a job in sales seemed like the perfect opportunity to improve on these skills. Little did I realize that this would be the point of no return.

Life as a new sales rep was difficult for me. There I was, going door-to-door, selling coupons for various restaurants and golf courses in Edmonton. Most of the time, I was sheepishly meandering through neighborhoods feeling sorry for myself, as I was pelted with rejections. And every now and then, my confidence would pick up when I heard a yes from a customer. I was on a constant emotional roller coaster.

- Customer: "No." (My thoughts: I suck at sales.)
- Next "No." (I told you, you suck at this.)
- "No." (I don't want to do this anymore.)
- "No." (I think I'm going to quit.)
- "No." (Is money even important anyway?)
- "Yes." (I can totally do this. I'm awesome.)
- Repeat over and over and over . . .

Six days a week, we had morning meetings and sales training. At the end of the training sessions, the experienced veterans would go into their last meeting of the day with the managers, and the rest of us new people would huddle in a circle and talk. I don't recommend this strategy to anyone trying to build sales teams. It was like *Lord of the Flies* as we, the new salespeople, were trying to figure things out.

We'd be in this circle and basically question our existence in the business. It was a discouraging way to finish the meetings and then enter the field. A few of the big topics we always circled around were, What are the chances of succeeding? What are the chances of advancing in this business? What percentage of people actually make it? We saw people around us quitting and dropping daily. It was a very difficult gig, and when you were paid on commission only, you felt not only the pain of rejection but also the struggle of living below the poverty line.

One morning a fellow new recruit named Kevin told me in our *Lord of the Flies* meeting that he was considering quitting. Kevin didn't strike me as a very ambitious guy, and he struggled in social settings. It seemed to me that Kevin was the wrong guy for this line of work, so I encouraged Kevin to look for a different job. It didn't take much arm-twisting; maybe I was better at sales than I thought. After Kevin quit, I thought, "How does Kevin quitting somehow affect my chances of succeeding in this business? Why would I allow myself to get discouraged or think my chances of success are somehow dependent on other people succeeding?" We spent a lot of time trying to calculate the law of averages of people succeeding based on the number of people we saw leave the business. Now Kevin was part of that statistics pool, and I thought it didn't make much sense that this guy who would inevitably quit could somehow affect my chance of success. Aren't my chances of success completely dependent on me? Aren't my chances of success completely independent of others? Think about flipping a coin. If I flip a coin, and nine times in a row it is tails, what are the chances that it's going to be heads on the tenth flip? It's an obvious mathematical answer: the chances still remain at 50 percent. The previous results have absolutely nothing to do with this next flip.

Fast-forward the clock years later. I'm running my business in Los Angeles, and I place an ad for "sports-minded" candidates to apply. I love working with athletes, as I believe athletes and businesspeople have similar mindsets—understanding what it takes to succeed (dedication, attitude, how to handle winning, how to handle losing, etc.). I was surprised when Danny Tartabull came in for an interview. Danny played fourteen years in MLB and had a very impressive career. In baseball he was an all-star and played for several teams, such as the Yankees, Royals, Phillies, and so on. On television, he made cameo appearances on *Seinfeld* and *Married... with Children*. Danny wasn't applying for a job because he needed the money; he was looking for purpose. He retired in his thirties, and in his early forties, he was looking for something to do. Danny and I hit it off, and we decided to work together.

I learned a lot from Danny. On one occasion, I commented that Danny was in such great shape. Even though he was wearing a suit and tie, it was obvious that he had a ton of muscles bulging out of his suit. I asked how often he hit the gym. His response was enlightening: "I still hit the gym six times per week. Habits are tough to break." This was the first time I heard someone say that great habits are tough to break.

On another occasion, Danny and I were having dinner late one evening, and I was asking him questions about his baseball days. I painted the following picture for him: "Okay, Danny, tell me what's going through your mind. You're up to bat. First of all, if you're awesome in the majors, you're getting on base one out of three times. Two out of three times, you're out. On this particular time at bat, you are going up against a pitcher that 'has your number.' Let's say that he has struck you out the last ten times at bat. What are you thinking? Do you have doubts? Are you still optimistic at the plate?"

Here was another one of Danny's enlightening comments to me: "Jaime, I'm telling you, every single time, no matter who the pitcher is or what kind of streak or slump I'm in, I am always thinking that I'm getting on base. There is never a doubt."

"Come on, Danny. My guess is that you probably *try* to think optimistically all the time, but this pitcher owns you. You're in a slump. Are you telling me that you're always thinking you're going to get on base no matter what?"

Danny held his ground. "Jaime, all of the great players that I played with over the years—McGwire, Canseco, etcetera—we all think like this. We will always get on base. There is never a doubt. You won't last long in the majors if you don't have this mindset."

Danny clearly understood "What are the chances?"

Think about the chances of succeeding in marriage. As a young man in my early twenties, this was a big concern of mine. It seemed like the chances of a failed marriage were about 40–50 percent. This statistic weighed heavily on my mind and possibly put me on a slower track for marriage, as I didn't want to become part of that statistic.

But how do other people's failed marriages affect our own

chances of success? Isn't each marriage unique and independent of the others? It's essential to realize that while statistics can provide general insights, they don't dictate our personal outcomes. Our individual choices, efforts, and attitudes play a far more significant role in determining the success of our relationships.

By focusing on our own growth, communication, and commitment, we can create a strong foundation for a successful marriage, regardless of external statistics or other people's experiences.

I hit a very critical point in this thinking: my chances of making it or not making it are either 100 percent or 0 percent. Either I was going to *decide* to make it, or I was going to *decide* to quit. There were no other numbers to consider. It's 100 or it's 0, nothing in between. The questions now were, What am I going to do? Can I commit and decide on the front end what outcome I want? Can I make sure that I maturely deal with the ebbs and flows of my emotional state? Is it as simple as making a decision?

Stephen Covey articulates it this way in *The 7 Habits of Highly Effective People*: "We are a product of neither nature nor nurture; we are a product of our choices, because there is always a space between stimulus and response." In other words, that space in between the stimulus (an event that evokes a reaction) and a response is the freedom to choose. Therefore, we should probably choose wisely.

As a young adult, I formed a decision-making process that played an incredibly important part in my journey. I encourage all readers to adopt this process to help you make good decisions and save yourself a lot of misery down the road. The decision-making process is as follows: make a decision on the front end, and then manage that decision on the back end. Making a good front-end decision means we need to avoid impulsive decision-making for the important things in life and avoid making decisions when we're emotional or unstable. Of course, we can make impulsive decisions for little things in life that require little thought. What am I going to eat today? What am I going to wear today? I'm talking about the important decisions in life (career, dating, where to live, values)—those that require a different level of commitment. Making a good front-end decision requires careful thought, sound logic, and a sense that you will commit to this regardless of the obstacles that you may encounter along this journey. If we don't make decisions and commitments on the front end, we will be vulnerable to life-changing decisions when we are at emotional lows. I've counseled several couples over the years who were struggling in their marriages, and the discussion of divorce came up. I often remind them, "Didn't you guys make a vow till death do you part? Didn't you make a lifelong decision on your wedding day—in sickness and in health, etcetera?" After bringing this up, I see people pause, reflect, and decide not to jump into hasty decision-making based on the current stress of the fractured relationship. Make the decision on the front end; manage that decision on the back end.

I want to end this chapter by pointing to a magical question that I ask mentors when it comes to making great decisions on the front end. "If you were me, what would you do?"

I have to tell you, when I get to a place where I've made a decision and I'm not going to look back, consulting with a mentor gives me a new gear of confidence in executing it because I know that I'm in good company. If this person whom I admire and strive to be like would also do what I'm about to do, then I believe I've made the right decision, and I can execute with confidence and conviction.

We've all heard, "All's well that ends well." I like reverse engineering that phrase a bit: all's well that begins well. I encourage you to be thoughtful on the front end, make great front-end decisions, and then manage those decisions on the back end. There will be less quitting, less starting over, and fewer redos. Our chances of success are really dependent on our front-end decisions. I truly believe that we are products of our decisions, not products of our circumstances.

My children have memorized a great quote from John Wooden that emphasizes this thought process: “There is a choice you have to make in everything you do. And you must always keep in mind the choice you make, makes you.”

Make great choices. All our chances and percentages are dependent on our decisions.

Chicken Little

As expressed in the introduction, JoAnne and I were expecting our first baby in 2009. This was such an exciting time for the both of us. One Saturday night, we were heading out for dinner and a movie. We were standing outside of the theaters in downtown Culver City. There were plenty of options to choose from, and I was gravitating toward all the action movies that I wanted to see—action, drama, speed—you know, the usual guy stuff. JoAnne (and her big baby belly) was also standing there, looking up at all the options in front of us. I asked her, "What would you like to see?" hoping she'd choose something in line with my interests. (Please don't pick your usual romantic comedy.)

"*Chicken Little*," she said.

"What? You're joking, right?"

"Everything other than *Chicken Little* has some sort of violence, sex, or adrenaline-producing scene in it. I don't want to pass any negative or scary emotions or adrenaline on to our baby."

I was stunned. I wasn't thinking like that. Weeks and even years later, it made me wonder about the effect that *anything* I allowed into my system was having on me.

Recently, I read an article regarding what we should all do in the event of an active shooter. I pray that none of us ever have to experience this. The article is intended to help readers be proactive and make good decisions in the midst of the chaos. There were several steps, but the first one really grabbed my attention. The first piece of advice is to "get down" or "get behind something." The author noted that "getting down" is obviously a no-brainer and that most readers would dismiss this advice. However, he observed that we live in a desensitized culture because of the explicit media, movies, video games, and so on that we are exposed to. Apparently, many victims in public shootings result from people watching the shooter and the madness happening around them. In the moment our brains are in shock from what we are witnessing, but having seen this kind of craziness on screens before, we want to watch to see how this plays out. In those early seconds, many people are unaware that this is real life and death. We want to watch and observe as if it were a movie. As the author studied the behaviors of survivors and those who perished, he argues that our society has blurred a vision between what's real and not real, and we can be paralyzed in these situations. So advice number one: get out of harm's way and don't stand still watching.

The point I'm trying to make is that we all have influences around us. We have screens in front of us most of the day with all kinds of information. We have people in our lives whom we like to be around and hang out with. We have our favorite shows to watch and favorite music and podcasts to listen to. It is worth our time and attention to think about this on the front end. Whom and what have you given permission to influence you?

What we allow into our lives will inevitably *make* us. I feel very lucky to be living in a time where literally anything we want to hear or watch is in little machines that we carry in our pockets. What powerful little beasts. It would be smart to let these little beasts influence for the better, not for the bitter. If we are all products of our decisions and the environments that we put ourselves in, then it makes sense to put ourselves in the best environments and states of mind available to us.

In 2016, I got caught up watching the primaries for the upcoming federal election. The conversations between these candidates were nothing less than verbal assaults. There were names called, insults, and many mean things thrown at each other. You know the cast of characters. I've always been somewhat of an information overload nerd, so I wanted to hear it all. Republican, Democrat, NBC, FOX, CNN, podcasts—everything. Then a well-needed "time-out" came along—the summer Olympics. Every two years I really enjoy watching the stories unfold in the Olympics. It's fascinating to learn about these extremely committed kids who have dedicated so much time and training for a few brief moments in time on the Olympic stage. Then, of course, as we get to know these athletes, we start cheering for them, loving them, and before we know it, the Olympics sweep us off our feet.

I didn't watch any political news coverage for the two weeks that the Olympics were on. I noticed a pretty big change in my psyche after the Olympics—I was simply happier. I didn't hear anyone calling each other names. I saw people hugging and celebrating. I was cheering for my two countries (Canada and the United States). Was it possible that something as simple as watching the news was making me pessimistic and upset? I think so.

In 2020, in the midst of the pandemic and the riots happening across the country, I once again found myself glued to the TV and social media. The country was divided on so many levels. It was really sad to see. But then something happened to me and my family—similar to the two weeks of the "Olympics time-out." We took a road trip across the country. We rented an RV and traveled from California to Colorado and then flew to Minnesota after that. We made plenty of stops along the way, meeting people at gas stations, campsites, restaurants, and national parks. We discovered something—Americans don't hate one another. The divide we saw on TV was not how it actually was out there. People were kind. People were friendly. People didn't care to know what your political beliefs were or where you stood on social issues. I needed that road trip time-out to realign my love for this country and refuel my "optimism tank."

The *Chicken Little* experience continues to creep into my life. It forces me to take inventory of my influences and to proactively choose the best influences that I allow to shape my mind, body, and spirit.

What and whom do you allow to form your trains of thought, beliefs, and values? Whether we realize it or not, we give permission to someone or something every time we surf the internet, watch TV, or listen to music. It might make sense to take an inventory of our influences and ask ourselves if we really want to give permission. We shouldn't underestimate the power of the environment around us. Whom and what will you allow to shape you? Choose wisely. Choose influences that aid your growth.

Do the Math

How do you look at the time you have in your day? I find it helpful to look at time from a different perspective to create positive habits in my life.

60 minutes per hour × 24 hours in a day =
1,440 minutes per day

If we divide those 1,440 minutes into 10-minute blocks, we have 144 blocks of time every day. Is it too much to ask of ourselves to invest one of those 144 blocks in personal growth? We can do whatever we want with the other 143 blocks of time. Just give one little block of time to personal growth (or anything that you are trying to make a priority). When I look at my day this way, it becomes very easy to invest one of these little blocks in myself. I can't really make an excuse to not give one of these blocks to my development.

A personal growth habit I easily adopted years ago was signing up for "Minute with Maxwell." For the last fifteen-plus years, I've watched a two-minute video from John Maxwell regarding his thoughts on a variety of subjects. Every week, five days per week, for fifteen-plus years. Essentially, I have given John Maxwell permission to shape me, to mold me, to make me think the way he thinks. This is an honor that I don't give to many people, but strategically, he is one of these "chosen mentors" of mine. He shapes my marriage, my business, my parenting, my attitude, my faith, my storytelling techniques, my presentation skills, and so on. Who is someone that you will strategically allow to shape your mind, body, and spirit? If you don't choose these people, the choice will be made for you randomly. This thought of choosing your influence was discussed in the previous chapter, "*Chicken Little*." This is where we apply this thought process. When it comes to Growing Right, many of us believe that we just don't have to dedicate to this journey. But "Do the Math" shows us that if we reframe our day by fractionalizing time, we will find that we do have the time.

Let's think about physical fitness for a second. I think most of us have struggled with getting enough exercise at various stages of our lives. Sometimes, we get in the habit and become dedicated; sometimes, we aren't so dedicated. I have found that when I "fall off my horse" with a lack of exercise, it's because I just don't have the time to block out two hours at the gym. But when I think about giving my physical health 1 of my 144 blocks of time, I can't really make an excuse. So I'll get into the habit of giving myself ten minutes each day of push-ups, stretching, sit-ups, and so on. A routine. Maybe I'll want to step this routine up a little bit and give myself 2 of these 144 blocks of time to exercise. You can see where this is going. The key is to create a good habit. Positive momentum is something to look for if you want to cement a good habit. I like little wins. Commit to something you know is easy to hit, such as giving yourself ten minutes per day, every day, to reading, working out, or whatever habit you're looking to cement. Every year, I set annual goals in multiple areas of my life, including physical fitness. I encourage others to do the same. If the commitment is too large, it'll be too easy to fall and drop it. How many times have we committed to "getting into shape" only to find ourselves doing nothing months later? What happened? Short answer: The commitment was too daunting.

I have found that most people set themselves up for failure by setting goals that are too high and require too much effort and commitment. It doesn't take long for discouragement to do its work when we don't feel like doing it anymore. After a few days of falling off the wagon, we start telling ourselves that we're failures, and we set ourselves up for that self-fulfilling prophecy.

I'll use physical goals to bring this point home. Most people start the year with their physical goals set too high. I once worked with a person who began the year with his game plan and goals. For his physical goals, he had written down, "Work out four days per week." I asked how often he hit the gym the previous year. He wasn't going to the gym at all. So I encouraged him to set the goal of going to the gym once per week. He was a little dumbfounded that I was encouraging him to set lower goals. I asked him if he could commit to going once a week, and he said, "Yes, obviously." I told him there is no shame in overachieving the goal. If you go four times a week, great. But if you only go once per week, you won't feel like a loser and get discouraged. He took this advice, didn't get down on himself for only showing up once per week at the gym, and eventually developed the routine and ritual of showing up multiple times a week. It's a lot easier to create a new habit with baby steps rather than large jumps. Large jumps have the power to sideline even the best of us.

Some will have the discipline to make these big lifestyle changes, but most don't. Discouragement does its work, and we're back to ground zero.

The trick is to form the habit. The trick is to feel good about yourself by underpromising and overdelivering. By fulfilling your goal, even if it is small, you will gain confidence. Confidence is key. You'll keep going. It'll cause a chain reaction. You'll probably increase the goal and commit to more since you're crushing the goal. Then you'll probably take that confidence into other arenas of your life that you're striving to be successful in.

If we commit and block off time for priorities in ten-minute increments, it's really difficult to justify not taking action. Surely we can all block off 1 of our 144 ten-minute blocks of time every day. Start there, get the wins, and then once you have the habit, you can "up the ante" and change it to two or three ten-minute blocks of time. Use the math to create the habit. Committing to one ten-minute block should be pretty simple and easy for all of us. If you're not a reader, you can ask yourself, "Can I commit to ten minutes per day to read?" It would be pretty hard to say no to that. Do this ten-minute exercise daily, and next thing you know, you've created the habit. Whether it's reading, exercise, or anything else, you're growing. You're growing right. You're growing right now.

I Want It All

Have you ever heard of the "sucker's choice"? It's a concept that says we must choose between this or that—the concept of "or." We can't always avoid "or" choices in life, but when we can, we should try to substitute "or" with "and."

My first recollection of being called out for sucker's choice was shortly after getting married. A friend of mine noticed that I had gained weight. He asked me about my weight gain, and I said, "I don't have time to work out. All of my time is dedicated to my business and my wife." He told me that I had a limiting belief and challenged me to look at my priorities differently. It was an incorrect statement to say that I didn't have time to work out. I have twenty-four hours per day just like everyone else. No one has more or less time. A more accurate statement would be, "It's just not a priority for me to work out and take better care of my health." (Ouch!)

And is the remedy for sucker's choice. I want a great career *and* a great marriage *and* great physical health *and* a great family life *and*...

There was a time in my life when I thought people had to eventually choose between being successful at home or being successful at work. I met many people who were doing well in their careers, but their family lives were unhealthy. I also met many people who were doing great with their family lives, but they lacked big-time career advancement. I think it can be said that most Americans are not living the balanced lives they wish they had.

However, I have found a growing number of people who do have it all. They are role models in multiple departments. I took the time to analyze my role models' habits to look for common denominators. I have found that these well-balanced role models avoid sucker's choice in their lives. If it's important, they'll carve out the time. If it's not important, they will find no time or energy for it. Again, we all have the same amount of time given to us daily. What are we doing with this time?

Years ago, I found myself feeling like I was spinning my tires with my business. It felt like I was putting in a lot of hours, but the business wasn't growing; we were stuck. I hired a consultant who specialized in priority management. He asked me to engage in one of the toughest exercises of my life. It was called the "Six-Minute Tracker." For two weeks, seven days per week, I had to write down what I was doing every six minutes. "I'm in the bathroom." Six minutes later, "I'm still in the bathroom." Six minutes later, "I'm on a call." Six minutes later, "I'm still on that call." You get the picture. Everywhere I went, the tracker tagged along. In my home, in my car, at my work, everywhere—I was scribbling down what I was doing. At the end of this daunting exercise, my consultant took all the data and categorized the events in my life that were consuming my time by separating them into their various priorities.

I'll spare you all the details of my findings, but I can tell you the big and final outcome of the exercise: 45 percent of my waking hours were spent doing important and meaningful things, and 55 percent of my waking hours were spent doing things that weren't important. Wow! I couldn't believe it. How could I be wasting so much time? I thought I was productive and doing important things.

An example of engaging in unimportant tasks is spending too much time on activities that should be completed quickly. The consultant tracked my calls, asked me to summarize the discussion, and then had me rate the importance of each call. If the call was important and we knew the issue at hand, it should have been relatively simple to resolve, making the call short. However, most of the time, the call droned on after the issue was solved, wasting valuable time. Many of these calls, which should have taken ten minutes, ended up lasting forty minutes instead.

Similarly, spending too much time on emails, browsing social media, or attending unnecessary meetings are other examples of unimportant tasks. On the other hand, tasks such as strategic planning, focusing on high-priority projects, and having meaningful conversations with key stakeholders are important and impactful.

Do this several times a day and you can see where hours are wasted. At this pace my life might end with many people shaking their heads, saying, "He had so much to give—too bad he wasted so much of his life." It kind of makes a guy want to cry.

Recognizing the difference between important and unimportant tasks is crucial. By prioritizing what truly matters, we can ensure that our time is spent in ways that lead to meaningful accomplishments and personal fulfillment.

How do I transfer the unimportant to the important? Intentionality. No one accidentally finds themselves on top of the mountain. A person must intentionally climb to get to the top. There is nothing fluky about it. I must intentionally slot important things into my calendar; otherwise, my calendar will unintentionally fill up with stuff, which may or may not be important, but why leave it to chance?

Years ago, I had a great conversation with a mentor of mine. This mentor is the most well-balanced, well-rounded person I know. In my opinion, he's winning in every important category (important to me) of his life: spiritual, marriage, fatherhood, business, philanthropy, and relationships. I told him that I felt like I was doing well in business *and* as a father but didn't feel like I was really winning in the role of a husband. He listened to me, as great mentors do, as I released some of my marriage frustrations. Then he said to me, "Jaime, I want it all. I don't want to have to compromise the most important things in my life. If it's important, then make it happen. Be a better husband. Be intentional. When you do your weekly planning, ask yourself, 'What can I do this week to be an awesome husband?'" Once again, I was humbled. The answer seems rather simple when you sit down and ponder why things that you think are priorities are slipping through the cracks. If intentions don't turn into actions, then we miss the mark. Knowing and not doing is not knowing. Consider a person who knows the importance of regular exercise for maintaining good health. They've read numerous articles, consulted with fitness experts, and even created a detailed workout plan. Despite having all this knowledge, they rarely exercise. Months go by and their health doesn't improve.

In this case, knowing the benefits of exercise and how to implement a fitness routine is useless if not acted upon. This illustrates the expression "Knowing and not doing is not knowing" because the true value of knowledge lies in its application. Without action, the person's understanding of the importance of exercise has no practical benefit, effectively nullifying their knowledge.

What does "I want it all" mean to you? Everyone will have a different answer to this question, and that's okay. What's important is that we invest our time in the things we value the most. The best way to gauge someone's values is to see where they spend their time and money. Where we spend our time and money screams loud and clear what matters to us. I've reflected many times on my own monthly financial transactions. There were times when I had to take a good look in the mirror after seeing multiple transactions for clothing and style and very few for charitable causes. My self-perception was that I was a good, caring person who prioritized helping others. However, with proper reflection, I was humbled to acknowledge that I was obviously more concerned with looking good than I was with helping others less fortunate than I. My checkbook revealed what was important to me. We tend to judge ourselves by our intentions, yet we judge others by their actions. Maybe we should evaluate ourselves by the same standards we use for others.

Let's take a good inventory of our values and reflect those values in our activities. This means we need to reverse engineer our approach to prioritizing. Until we get proactive, our values will be revealed in our calendars and checkbooks, after our decisions have already been made. I'd rather think of the values and important things in life up front and then make sure my decisions reflect them. It's a lot easier to say no to the important things in life that consume our time when we're proactive. We *can* have it all. It is a limiting belief to think otherwise. Now that we know we don't have to sacrifice the things that we value, let's figure out how to identify what "having it all" means to you.

Bananas, Dry Cleaning, and Mom

John Maxwell's introduction at his *Today Matters* seminar left a mark on me. It went something like this:

"Give me twenty-four hours to observe you. I want to be by your bedside early in the morning before you wake up. I'll have my pen and notepad with me all day to observe and take notes. I promise not to bother you. I want to see what you do, your routines, how you go about your day. I want to be with you in your car as you drive to work, observe what you listen to, and try to see how you're thinking about things. I want to observe you at work and watch how you interact with people, how often you're online, what you're doing online, observe your focus with which you do your work. I'll ride home with you after work, watch you interact with your family and friends, and take note of what your home activities are. I'll be with you as you get ready for bed, and as you lay your head on your pillow and close your eyes, I'll take my last notes. At the end of it all, I will be able to tell beyond a shadow of a doubt whether you'll go on to be a huge success in life or whether you'll go on to be a huge failure. The answer lies in your daily agenda."

Since then, I have been obsessed with making the best use of my time, trying my best to avoid wastefulness, and exploring the latest and greatest tools to help me stay on track.

I was lucky enough to have lunch with John Maxwell and ask him how he manages his priorities and stays on track. He has a lot going on in his life with his family, travels, speaking engagements, businesses, writing, and nonprofit work. His answer was fascinating and unique. John told me that he and his trusted assistant, Linda, block off two full days to plan the next forty days of his life. These two full days are dedicated to making sure that all of John's priorities and the people important to him are properly integrated into his life. They'll get into the details of each grandchild, each speaking engagement and the audience, everything. He doesn't leave his calendar up to chance. He is very intentional about scheduling his highest priorities. John and others proved to me that successful people don't prioritize their schedules; they schedule their priorities.

Despite the abundance of tools and resources available, many individuals fail to utilize their calendars to their full potential. Instead of serving as structured road maps for their days, calendars often become cluttered with nonessential tasks or, worse, remain underutilized. This lack of effective calendar management leads to missed deadlines, forgotten appointments, and a general sense of disorganization. By addressing this issue and implementing strategies for better calendar use, we can significantly improve productivity and time management.

I often ask people to show me their system for keeping track of their priorities. There are a couple of reasons for this: First, they might have a better way of doing it than I, so maybe there is something I can learn. Second, they might need an improved system, and I can equip them with some of my tools and latest systems. One day, one of my coworkers asked me for help and wanted advice and coaching. He was struggling with work and was stressed out at home as well. He felt like he was losing on both fronts. In the spirit of Maxwell's seminar, I asked him if we could look at his calendar together to see how he was spending his time.

He was having a difficult time connecting how his calendar had anything to do with his problems at home and his inefficiencies at work. I told him that his calendar would tell us what was most important to him and might help him reflect on his priorities and juggle some things around. He opened up his calendar app on his phone so we could see if there were any indicators or clues that we should explore. Over the course of the last 168 hours (24×7), he had three things plugged into his calendar: "Bananas" on Tuesday, "Dry Cleaning" on Saturday, and "Call Mom" on Sunday. I asked him if he had accomplished all the things that he prioritized in his calendar. He didn't really understand the question. I then asked him specifically, "Did you buy your bananas, pick up your dry cleaning, and call your mom?"

He nodded, saying, "Yes."

"Then I guess that you're on the right track. You're setting your sights on things, and you are executing those things. You have the habit of following through on the things that you set out to do. That's great!"

"Uh, okay," he said.

"If you want to accomplish more with your life, why don't you think of the things that are important and plant them in your calendar too? I'm not sure how long it took you to get the bananas, the dry cleaning, and call your mom, but I would think you probably have another 166 hours or more per week to get other stuff done."

"Well, those other things I don't write down. I know what they are, and I do them," he said.

"You might be right. You might be wrong. I don't know. All I know is those other things are probably much more important than bananas. If bananas can find their way onto your calendar, just try putting the other things in your calendar, and let's see what happens."

I'm happy to report that he took the advice to heart, got in the habit of scheduling his priorities, and turned the ship around at work and at home. Because he took the time to clearly lay out what was important to him, it was harder for more trivial things to take up his time and distract him from what he really cared about.

Years ago, I told a friend that my life felt like I was driving on ice. The speedometer said 100 mph, but in reality it felt like I was only going 10 mph. My tires were spinning, and I didn't know why I was not really getting ahead. I asked him if he ever felt like that.

He just listened and didn't offer me any advice. Then months later he told me that he was going to send me to a time management seminar. The seminar happened to fall on a Monday—Mondays were very busy for me. I started to respond, "I really appreciate it, but I'm too busy for a time management . . ." Then I stopped myself and thought, "I don't have *time* for a *time* management course? I think I might have discovered my problem."

I have found that if we are not intentional with our time, the unimportant things in life have the cunning ability to sneak in and consume our clocks. Have you ever been internet surfing, watching shows or movies, texting, talking on the phone, or playing video games and come out of your little session surprised at how much time has passed? Are you surprised when you go to your phone's settings, look at your screen time, and see how much time that device is taking from you? Are you surprised when you look at the details of which apps take the majority of your time? Our time is eaten up every day, and if we're not careful or intentional, it can be eaten up by the less important things.

The discipline of the Six-Minute Tracker, which was discussed in the previous chapter, revealed that I was a victim of wasting 55 percent of my waking hours. I'd rather not have my priorities exposed to me by doing another Six-Minute Tracker. It makes a lot more sense to me to be proactive, plug my priorities into my calendar, and treat them like appointments—appointments with the gym, appointments with important relationships, appointments with high-value tasks at work. When it's an appointment, it tends to get done. When it's not an appointment, it has the tendency to be a good idea but doesn't translate into execution.

As discussed in "I Want It All," I was subpar, in my opinion, as a husband. When I decided to do something about it, I asked myself, "What can I do this week to be an awesome husband?" When I'm in my "planning mode" for the upcoming week, my role as a husband comes up. "This week, what can I do? What actions can I take to make my wife feel like she is the center of my universe? How can I make her feel loved, valued, and the most important person in my life?" Think about it: Just framing it that way, thinking of my role as a husband that way, asking those kinds of questions, how can I lose? Of course, not only do I need to come up with some great answers to those questions, but I also need to turn them into action and plant them in my calendar. Again, if bananas can make it onto a written list, how can my wife not take precedence? Is the reason that most of us do not write this stuff down that we overestimate ourselves and neglect the action because we know we have good intentions? It's certainly possible. Write it down. Should I bring home flowers? Should I write her a little note? When we have time to talk, what's important to her? What kind of conversation lights her up? I'm happy to say that my report card (self-report card, that is) in the role of a husband has improved dramatically, as my wife testifies. There aren't many things in life that motivate me more than knowing that I'm succeeding as a husband. It's hard to believe that I used to make excuses about a "lack of time" for something that's so important to me.

After all my studies over the years, I have the following key takeaways to share:

1. There is no such thing as controlling time. We can only manage what we do with it. None of us can manage time; we have no control. We cannot slow it down, nor can we speed it up. Time just keeps ticking, and there's nothing

we can do about it. The better term to use is "priority management." That is something in our control, not time. So we need to think about our time in terms of priorities and ideally spend it engaged in the most important and highest-valued activities throughout the week.

2. When we identify our values and what's most important, it becomes a lot easier to say no to things that don't matter. Think about it: we can only say yes to one thing at a time. As I'm writing this, I am saying yes to sitting down with my computer and sharing these stories. That means I'm saying no to everything else—TV, sports, my family, my gym time—everything. When I put it in those terms, am I sure I should be spending the time saying yes to this one task? Lucky for me, at this moment, I'm on a plane traveling from a work trip, so I don't have the option to spend time with my wife or my kids. Soon enough I'll see them, and when I do, I'll be saying no to everything else, including the writing of this book. We say yes to one thing and no to a million other things. I have learned that saying no is empowering and peaceful because it means I am saying yes to something important.

3. I learned a little history on the word "priority." Priority has a Latin origin, and it entered the English language in the 1400s. It means prior, former, or first. It was a singular word, and it remained so until the 1900s. Our culture pluralized it shortly after the industrial boom, and we started talking about "priorities." Now we have multiple first things. It doesn't really make much sense, does it? How can we have multiple first things? Isn't there only one first thing? Shouldn't we go back to singularizing the word to keep its true origin? Knowing this history has caused me

to reflect and ask the questions, How many priorities do I have? Can I narrow them down to one? Since I do have multiple priorities, can I rank them from most important to least important? Can I simplify and limit the priorities so I can focus on just a small number? By doing this, I'm hoping to be more productive and better at fewer but more important things.

Once we have the priority or priorities identified, they can be transformed into great execution by plugging them into our calendars every week.

4. We overestimate our memories. We don't think we need to write the important things down or be meticulous with our calendars because we already know what's important. Like my friend who used the calendar for his bananas, dry cleaning, and mom, we often mistake the calendar for something like a grocery list. In reality, a proactive calendar is needed to make sure you don't slip into what Stephen Covey calls the "quadrant of deception"—engaging in activities that are urgent but not important. Your buttoned-up calendar is a necessary weapon against the deception of what we think is a productive life.

You Don't Choose Your Values

At a FranklinCovey class, I met one of my favorite instructors—Hoac. Hoac was a Green Beret, and he commanded authority and respect. I really enjoyed listening to him, and I loved his style. I loved it, until he said something to me that was very disturbing. He said, "You don't choose your values. Your values are exposed through your daily decisions."

He made this comment shortly before a fifteen-minute recess. I think Hoac knew people would have a visceral reaction to the comment, "You don't choose your values." I don't think it was by fluke that a short recess followed such a controversial statement. I couldn't help but ponder this thought, so I went up to Hoac during the break and told him that I questioned that logic. I believed that, of course, we all choose our values. He said that most people don't take the time to think about their values; therefore, their values are simply exposed by their decisions.

After the break, Hoac brought our conversation up for the group. He asked if anyone else was bothered with his comment, "You don't choose your values." I think because of his military background, people reluctantly put their hands up—they didn't really want to challenge his authority.

Hoac said, "If you don't like this paradigm, then you must reengineer your life. You must take the time to think through your values and create a clarifying statement for each one. Identify what's important to you and why it's important. Most people never do the exercise I'm about to give you, but I'll tell you, if you do it, it'll change your life. You have forty-eight hours after this class ends to clearly identify your values and produce a clarifying statement for each value. The number of values doesn't matter. All that matters is that you think through this and gain clarity on your values. You'll see that the decision-making that follows will be aligned with your values."

I was convinced, so I spent the next couple of days with a paper and pen, asking myself what I value. This is not an easy exercise; it forces you to think through and evaluate what's important to you.

Here are a few examples of values and clarifying statements that I came up with:

- Gratitude—Be thankful for what I have, not envious of what I don't have. Gratitude and envy cannot coexist in the same heart.
- Freedom—It's not my ability to choose that makes me free. It's the decisions that I make within that freedom that make me free.
- Forgiveness—I will not hold grudges on anyone. I will be quick to forgive and forget.
- Family and friends—Create special moments and memories with special people.

My first draft had seventeen values. My current list has thirty. A few years ago, I was lucky to meet Ken Blanchard and talk to him about values. He encouraged me to shorten my list to three or four values. He's a Christian man and gave me a great biblical reference. He said that the children of Israel were given ten values (commandments) to live by, and then Jesus showed up on the scene and simplified them to two core godly values. I liked that reference.

I came up with my core values (now my family values) using the acronym LIFE: Leadership, Integrity, Faith, and Excellence. And of course I have a clarifying statement for each one of these.

I encourage you to spend the time now—Grow Right Now—to identify what's important to you. Identify your values, and create a clarifying statement. When you plug your priorities into your calendar, you will feel a sense of satisfaction and fulfillment knowing that your activities are rooted in your values.

Every month for the last fifteen years, I make the time to reread the poem "Slow Dance," by David L. Weatherford. It helps me reflect and ask myself if I need to reevaluate my priorities and values.

At its core, "Slow Dance" is a gentle reminder to embrace the present moment and resist the urge to rush through life. The poem utilizes vivid imagery and metaphors to convey this message:

- The dance metaphor: Life is likened to a slow dance, emphasizing the importance of savoring each step and movement. Rushing through the dance would mean missing out on its beauty and intimacy.
- "The music is playing" and "the world is waiting": These lines highlight the contrast between the external world's demands and the internal experience of being present. The world can wait while we engage in the dance of life.
- "For a song that will never come again": This poignant phrase underscores the fleeting nature of life and the importance of cherishing each moment as it unfolds.
- "Give it to someone special": The poem encourages us to share these precious moments with loved ones, creating meaningful connections and memories.

Why should we revisit the message? In today's fast-paced world, the message of "Slow Dance" is perhaps more relevant than ever. We are constantly bombarded with information, notifications, and demands on our time. It's easy to get caught up in the rush and forget to appreciate the simple joys of life.

Revisiting this poem reminds us to:

- Prioritize presence: By slowing down and focusing on the present moment, we can experience life more fully and deeply.
- Cultivate gratitude: Taking the time to appreciate the good things in our lives can foster a sense of contentment and well-being.
- Nurture relationships: Sharing special moments with loved ones strengthens our bonds and creates lasting memories.
- Resist the rush: The world will keep spinning, but we have the power to choose how we engage with it. We can step off the treadmill and savor the dance of life.

"Slow Dance" offers a timeless message about the importance of presence, gratitude, and connection. In a world that often encourages us to hurry, this poem invites us to slow down, breathe, and truly live.

Hoac was right; your values are exposed in your daily decisions. *But* you choose your priorities. You own them. Aligning our priorities with our values lets our branches grow from the right tree. Just as branches can only grow strong and healthy on a well-chosen tree, your priorities will thrive when they are rooted in your core values. Identifying our values lets us Grow Right.

Grow. Grow Right. Grow Right Now.

Over the years I developed a mission statement for my business, which focuses on developing young professionals in sales to grow into leadership and management capacities. The mission statement is this:

"Grow. Grow Right. Grow Right Now."

GROW

In my business we are all expected to grow—personally and professionally. In fact, if you want to grow professionally, I would argue that a person's professional growth curve is right behind their personal growth curve; professional growth is directly proportional to personal growth. If the personal curve isn't going up, then I would not expect the professional curve to go up. It is very possible to flatline in any career if the personal growth curve is neglected.

You know you're on the road to success because it's uphill all the way. If you're in a car and you take your foot off the gas, the best-case scenario is you won't go anywhere. The worst-case scenario is you can slide backward. To move forward, the throttle must be pushed. I think all professions should be treated like IT or medicine. If you're in either of these industries and you're not constantly studying and keeping up with the times, you become obsolete.

I have a friend in IT who works full time *and* studies thirty-plus hours per week just to keep up with the changing times. If you are always trying to reinvent yourself and become better, you will find success in any industry.

Our personal growth is something that we must each own. It might have been something that our teachers and bosses owned in our early years, but that lack of proactivity ends today. No one should care more about our personal growth than us. The two most important days in our lives are the day we were born and the day we realize why we were born—finding the purpose or the cause of our lives. Owning our personal growth puts us on the path to learning our why, our passion, and the reason we were put on this planet. It wasn't just by chance, so don't leave your personal growth up to chance. Own it. Grow.

GROW RIGHT

How do people feel about us when they are around us? How do people feel about themselves when they are around us? I think if we're "growing right," others will feel good about themselves and love being around us. People will sense the genuineness and love for others in us if we are growing right.

As discussed in the previous chapter, I went through the exercise of identifying my values and creating a clarifying statement for each value. I noticed that I had a disconnect with what I had written down and what reality was. It looked pretty good on paper, and it's who I *wanted* to be, but it wasn't always who I was. The problem is that I am a piece of work and always "under construction," and many times I found that I fell short of my own expectations. One of my values on that paper is "Health—to be healthy in all four areas of my life—physical, social/emotional, mental, and spiritual." Sounds good. Looks good. However, believe it or not, I was smoking the occasional cigarette from time to time. I eventually had to have a critical conversation with myself and decide what I was going to do. Either I change the value to "Be healthy in three areas of my life" and remove the physical part *or* I remove the cigarettes. I didn't want to be a hypocrite with this value any longer. The reality was that I didn't value my physical health. I was lying to myself.

I just couldn't hit the backspace button and remove physical health as a value, so I worked hard on kicking the awful habit of smoking and eventually succeeded. I continuously work on the "Hepp Values." I reflect on them monthly. I adjust and tweak them often. I put them in a frame in my home office. My kids look at them and ask questions about them, and now they are creating their own values and mission statements. I have more pressure now to fulfill this wonderful list of values and try to be a role model for my family, my coworkers, and my community. I want that pressure. I want to Grow Right.

If we pursue growth but we aren't sensitive to honorable attributes such as integrity, servant leadership, and honesty, we could put ourselves in a real mess.

Imagine this: You're cutting corners or stepping on others to advance, and you actually do find yourself succeeding. However, what a shame it would be if, after many years of climbing the branches of the tree of success, you realize you've been climbing the wrong tree all along. Each branch you ascended, thinking it would bring you closer to your goals—the fruit—turns out to have led you away from your true values and purpose. Instead of thriving in the rich soil of integrity and meaningful achievement, you find yourself at the top of a barren tree, with nothing substantial to hold on to. An example of this could be driving our careers and work advancement at the expense of losing the most important relationships in our lives. In a case like this, we are climbing the branches of a tree built solely on achievement and ambition. But this is the wrong tree. Climbing the branches of a tree rooted in steady and meaningful relationships will allow us to stabilize our growth as we reach for our ambitions. Can we really define someone with status and money but poor character and no sincere relationships as successful? In my opinion, no.

As we commit to growing, it is important that we commit to growing right. An indicator that we're growing right is very simple: other people's lives improve because of your growth. Other people benefit. Others experience a better quality of life because of you. If you're the only one benefiting, there's a good chance you're not growing right. The branches we climb should not only support our ambitions but also foster and enhance the lives of those around us.

GROW RIGHT NOW

In my business we are all expected to Grow Right Now—*today*. Today is where action lies.

The past and the future are not in our control; there is no taking action in the past or the future. The present is the only time action can occur. Master Oogway in *Kung Fu Panda* articulates this thought well: "Yesterday is history, tomorrow is a mystery, but today is a gift. That's why it's called the present." To me, being present is being aware and being active simultaneously.

Another saying that I've taught my kids is, "You can do the right thing or the easy thing." Of course, that makes a child stop and say, "Don't you mean that you can do the right thing or the wrong thing?" Exactly. The easy thing *is* the wrong thing.

What's easier—eating chocolate cake or eating green beans?

What's easier—forgiving someone or seeking revenge after they've hurt you?

What's easier—watching TV or going to bed?

What's easier—waking up early or staying in a nice, warm bed?

Easy can become the enemy. Create the habit of making the tough choices, whether they are small or big. Eventually, the right thing becomes the "easier thing" with the right character. Growing in character creates a powerful will. All this growing is necessary with the power of now, the power of today. I often remind my kids of the "Procrastinator's Credo," which states, "Tomorrow is always the best day to get something done." Procrastinators choose easy. "Grow. Grow Right. Grow Right Now." brings a sense of urgency to decision-making.

Abraham Lincoln said, "Things may come to those who wait, but only the things left by those who hustle." I said this earlier: "Knowing without doing is not knowing." Action is a necessary ingredient for growing right.

Make Today Your Masterpiece

When it comes to career options for my children, I'm not pushing them in any particular direction. We often discuss their strengths and passions, which are great indicators of where they might want to invest their time and energy. However, what I emphasize more is striving toward excellence. I tell them repeatedly that I just want to see them try their best in whatever they choose to do. If they strive for excellence and become part of the top 5 percent in their field, success in the form of money, promotions, and advancement will naturally follow. But if their best doesn't equate to being in the top 5 percent, that's perfectly okay too. What matters most is that they put forth their greatest effort and take pride in their work, knowing they have given it their all.

Whenever anything in our home is done half-heartedly, we always joke that maybe we should change the Hepp Values to LIFM—Leadership, Integrity, Faith, and Mediocrity. We don't have to adhere to the standard of excellence, but LIFM does sound a little strange. The kids will laugh at my humor, and then they'll recommit to doing things right—doing them with excellence. So far, no one has bought into changing the values to LIFM.

What I want to pass down to my children about the value of excellence is "Make Today Your Masterpiece." This is a line that stuck with me when I had the privilege of seeing UCLA men's basketball coach, John Wooden, speak at a seminar. Coach Wooden had an impressive résumé at UCLA—his teams won ten NCAA national basketball championships in a twelve-year time frame as the head coach of the Bruins. He was a winner, and his players valued their time with him. He coached many of the greats who would change the game of basketball, such as Kareem Abdul-Jabbar and Bill Walton. John Wooden was *the* model for me. His coaching style, attention to detail, and deep love for his players were qualities I wanted to emulate.

I compare my profession to that of an NCAA sports coach. I coach and develop young business professionals in sales, leadership, entrepreneurship, finances, and business. Some of my students go on to do big things and run very successful companies within the organization; others find themselves with me for a short season and move on to other careers. Either way, my job is to add value to everyone on the team and help people achieve greatness. Sounds like the role of college coaches, doesn't it? A small percentage of people go on to the pros; everyone else eventually moves on to industries and jobs outside the sport they were playing at college.

Coach Wooden had the credibility to be on stage after his coaching career with UCLA to teach the world about leadership. He shared the stage with some of the best leaders from around the country from diverse political and business backgrounds. Wooden's track record in the NCAA was certainly admirable, but I found some of the best John Wooden stories out there happened off the court. Several of John's players revealed that they learned more about marriage than they ever did about basketball. What? Hang on a second. UCLA paid Wooden to coach basketball, to win games, to bring in big revenue for the school. They did not pay him to counsel young men on marriage, yet here were these boys learning how to value their future spouses, not just how to win on the basketball court.

Coach Wooden's "Pyramid of Success" is worth studying. It outlined the blueprint of what he wanted each player to experience at UCLA. Using the blocks of the pyramid, he intentionally and specifically identified the characteristics and traits that define a successful person. Two of these pyramid blocks—the cornerstones—are industriousness and enthusiasm. These two blocks are critical in putting the other blocks in place. You need industriousness, the work ethic, to master your craft and become great. It's a lot like the "ten-thousand-hour rule"—to be considered an expert, you need to invest ten-thousand-plus hours into a skill or craft. You also need the enthusiasm and passion to be present. The enthusiasm will give you the energy to go through the ups and the downs. Every other block is supported by these two important blocks.

As you study his pyramid and blocks, you'll come away with one of Wooden's greatest lessons that I've adopted in my own life: Make Today Your Masterpiece. This was part of the daily regimen of sharpening the right mindset. Today is here for a small moment of time, and then it's gone, never to return. We can dwell on the past, and we can look forward to the future. But the real power is in the present. The present is where the action is. Knowing is never enough. Doing has the power; applying knowledge has power. Why not make today a masterpiece? Why not make it as good as it could possibly be? "Grow. Grow Right. Grow Right Now." embodies the value of excellence.

Years ago, I was going through the drive-through at the Coffee Bean at the early hour of 6:00 a.m. I'd been in this habit for years, and nothing was out of ordinary—except the person who greeted me over the intercom one day. The person, John John, greeted me with an enthusiastic "Good morning!" I surprisingly responded back with "Well, you're rather perky this morning." He said, "Yes, of course. It's a great day to be alive and loving the day." Again, all this was expressed in the most enthusiastic voice you can imagine.

I ordered my coffee, got to the window, and gave him a business card. I told John John that I wanted to hire him and work with him even though I didn't know anything about him. I just wanted that kind of excellence in my business—in any capacity. If he was like this at a coffee shop, imagine how awesome he would be in sales, leadership, and developing people.

I ended up hiring John John and becoming friends with him. I was curious how often he was "noticed" and offered jobs.

"All of the time. I received job offers every day. I looked at my job at the Coffee Bean as my auditions to be an actor or get noticed by bosses. I never knew who was who, but I figured the law of averages would work out, and I'd eventually get discovered."

Well, John John was noticed, all right. He was a great example of Making Today Your Masterpiece. After working with John John, I started paying closer attention to everyone I encountered at every job I had exposure to—the baristas, the mechanics, the sandwich artists, the salespeople, the managers, the police officers, the nurses, the lawyers, the pastors, the flight attendants, the athletes, the businesspeople, the janitors, the authors, the brokers, and so on. Along my journey, I discovered that we have an interesting way of conflating effort and passion. It seems our culture embraces the attitude and paradigm that only if they are passionate about something will they then give tremendous effort. In other words, if the passion isn't there, "masterpiece" would be a little too strong to describe the day.

Think about this: At every turn we see people giving half-hearted efforts at their crafts. Those who give everything to their craft are often seen as weird—just as I'm sure John John's fellow employees saw him. People criticize great effort, especially for doing a task that some might consider menial. It doesn't make sense to most people that effort can come without some sort of passion. You don't need to love everything you do to do it well. We must not become vulnerable to judgment.

People are a lot like crabs. If you want to boil crabs, you don't have to put a lid on the pot. When one crab tries crawling out of the pot, the other crabs will grab it and pull it back in. Funny how human nature is the same. As you Make Today Your Masterpiece, be prepared for the other crabs to try to bring you back into the pot of mediocrity.

I have a few logical arguments for why effort should always come before passion. First, how are we supposed to know all the things we are passionate about? I was clueless that I had a passion to serve people through selling. I never would have known this if I hadn't tried new things with an enormous amount of effort. I was nervous and unproductive as a salesperson. However, over time, I learned that people often lacked the time to do a lot of research, creating a need for a really good salesperson who could serve them and sell with integrity. I also liked making people smile, being a ray of sunshine for them, whether they bought or not. I ended up loving sales. Who would have known that? Effort showed up first, and then a new passion was exposed.

I was also clueless that I had a passion to lead people. I didn't consider myself a leader in school, yet I absolutely loved being in a position of influence for young trainees when I first started my career. Again, effort preceded passion.

Second, effort makes you "discoverable," just like the Bluetooth on your phone. Your phone is trying to discover new devices to connect to. Similarly, companies are engaged in recruiting wars, trying to acquire the best talent around. Most companies struggle in this department, as it's competitive to get the best and brightest to join their causes. Being discoverable opens doors. Instead of you doing the searching, being discoverable means opportunities will come knocking on your door. John John had several people like me knocking on his door.

Lastly, let's just look at basic physics. The amount of effort it takes to move a stationary ball is greater than the amount of effort it takes to redirect a ball already in motion. If the habits of effort and enthusiasm are already in motion, you will not only discover what you are passionate about, but you will also be equipped with the energy and skills to pursue it. Think of the opposite situation. What a tragedy it would be if you finally found your passion, only to discover that you are ill-equipped with the proper skill set and mindset to really be excellent at your passion. You're ill-equipped because you have conditioned yourself to only put in minimal effort. You don't have the habits or confidence to give something your best. You've cemented the devastating habit of mediocrity. Coach Wooden would tell his players that they should expect to play like they practice. If they give it a 70 percent effort in practice, they should expect to play at 70 percent during the game. It is illogical to think that you can "turn it on" and give it 100 percent when you've conditioned yourself to give 70 percent. It's even more illogical to think that you can give 130 percent effort to make up for the 70 percent effort during practice. Wooden used to call Bill Walton when Walton was a commentator for ESPN/ABC during NBA games. Wooden would politely correct Walton when he would make comments such as, "He's giving 110 percent out there," by saying, "Now, Bill, the most anyone can ever give is 100 percent. No one can give more than that."

Wooden used to say, "It's too late for preparation when opportunity strikes." Of course, that makes sense in sports. If we haven't practiced the specific plays and skills in practice, what would make us think we'll properly execute a skill when the need suddenly arises in the big game? But basketball is just a microcosm of what life has in store for us. What a shame if our opportunities in life fall into our laps and we find ourselves unprepared. What a shame if we've cemented habits of mediocrity. It doesn't matter what you do; do it with excellence. I challenge anyone to tell me that they pursued something they weren't passionate about with excellence and ended up regretting it. You won't regret putting effort first before passion.

It might seem illogical that we should all be preparing for our dream jobs by giving our best effort all the time, especially if our current position doesn't provide us a lot of enthusiasm or passion. I would challenge us to look at the "nondream jobs" as dress rehearsals. If you can give the boring, mundane, and non-passionate work your very best effort, imagine how great you'll execute when you are engaged in your passions. Make Today Your Masterpiece. Use today to Grow Right Now.

Find a Mentor

It's been said that it takes a village to raise a child. As a father of three, I know this to be true. JoAnne and I rely on an army of wonderful people who love our family and take an active interest in our development. Think of all the roles that make up your "supporting cast"—all the people who share your life's journey. We all have teachers, friends, and family, but what about mentors? Do you have mentors in your life?

A quick Google search for "mentor" yields this definition: "an experienced and trusted advisor." The importance of having mentors cannot be overstated. They are the guiding branches in the tree of our success, helping us navigate the complexities of growth and development. Just as we need strong roots and supportive branches to Grow Right, having mentors ensures that our climb is steady, enriching, and aligned with our true values. In this chapter we'll explore the critical role mentors play in our lives and how they can help us grow not just upward but also in all the right directions.

Does everyone need a mentor? No. A mentor is only necessary for those who want to improve. Do you sense a little sarcasm with my response to this question? It surprises me how many people don't seek mentorship. I think this lack of pursuit comes from a few different places, such as the following:

1. We are indifferent. We aren't really looking to level up; we are content with where we are.
2. We lack self-awareness and are unaware of how much improvement is needed.
3. We are overconfident that things will turn out in our favor as long as we keep going.
4. We are insecure. Why would this person who's doing so well in life want to spend time with me?

INDIFFERENCE ISSUE

How does one identify and battle the feeling of indifference? I would think that halfway through this book, this no longer describes you. I believe the remedy for indifference is ambition. If you lack ambition, you must think bigger. Tony Robbins said something years ago that really made me think: "People are not lazy. They simply have impotent goals—that is, goals that do not inspire them." Find the goal, find the passion, find the purpose. A person of purpose is not indifferent. They play to win.

At some point in time, we will all be forced to level up. Life changes way too fast to get comfortable. Tap into your ambitious nature.

LACK OF SELF-AWARENESS ISSUE

It takes a lot of courage and humility to ask others for their opinions and criticism. Questions such as, "Are there any areas in my life that you think I could improve? How do you see me? How do others see me?" are not easy to ask. Do you really want to hear the answers to tough questions like that? I've found that when my concern for my future is greater than my ego, I become very open to criticism.

Norman Vincent Peale put it this way: "The trouble with most of us is that we'd rather be ruined by praise than saved by criticism." We avoid criticism because it doesn't feel good. We feel judged and low. This is often a result of insecurity, where we fear that criticism will expose our weaknesses and make us feel unworthy. Insecurity causes us to avoid feedback because it threatens our self-esteem.

On the other hand, a lack of self-awareness means we might not even recognize our need for improvement. We might be oblivious to our shortcomings and dismiss criticism as irrelevant or unjustified. While insecurity is about fearing exposure, a lack of self-awareness is about being blind to our own faults.

It comes back to the big word—priorities. What's more important to you: improvement and success or not feeling bad? If improvement is what you're seeking, then you might not find any tool more powerful than human-to-human contact and critique with a person you trust, respect, and admire. I refer to these people as my "wise council." Embracing their feedback helps bridge the gap between insecurity and self-awareness, leading to meaningful growth and development. By valuing their insights, you can overcome insecurity and gain the self-awareness needed to truly improve.

OVERCONFIDENCE ISSUE

I'm a big fan of hope. I am a hopeful and optimistic person. I will say, however, that if hope is your only strategy and plan, then you might be wildly disappointed as you age. Additionally, it seems too risky to leave your success up to a feeling of hope. You might fall short of your financial dreams, relationship goals, or any other priority that you're hoping to succeed at. I suggest combining hope with great decision-making, accountability, and action. Ironically, you'll find confidence really skyrocketing with great mentorship because you'll find yourself engaged in activities where you'll ask yourself, "What would my mentor do?" As you move and attempt to execute your plan, you'll be engaged with more enthusiasm and confidence (even though you might fail) because you know that your mentor would be doing the exact same thing you're doing if they were in your shoes.

INSECURE ISSUE

The biggest value that doing door-to-door sales brought me was the destruction of my insecurities. It was terrifying to knock on doors, be belittled, and experience rejection hundreds of times per month. Eventually, you learn a few things along the way. Here are a few of them:

- A business refusal is not the same as personal rejection. As a new salesperson, I took the rejection personally. I thought people were saying no to me. One of my trainers helped me adjust my mindset when he brought up the difference between a business refusal and a personal rejection. A business refusal is someone saying no to your product or service. Personal rejection happens when someone denies you because of who you are—your character. That paradigm shift helped me a lot, as I no longer took rejection to heart. Don't confuse the two.
- You're probably never going to see these people ever again, so why do you care about what they think or say? Years ago, I was in Hollywood with a group of people, and we saw Shooter McGavin (a *Happy Gilmore* character) sitting at the bar. Only two of us approached him to meet him and take a picture. The others were a little shy to go meet him. The way I looked at it, what were the chances of me ever meeting Shooter McGavin again? Probably close to 0 percent. Thanks to my squashed fear of rejection, I now send a photo of Shooter and me to several of my

appreciative golfing buddies.

- You only fail when you fail to try. As Wayne Gretzky said, "You miss 100 percent of the shots you don't take." Every failure brings you one step closer to success, so learn to take the no and don't get deflated along the way. Keep your esteem in check. Protect your confidence.

We have to learn to get over our insecurities and lose the fear that a potential mentor might reject our request. As Julius Caesar said, "Fortune favors the bold." Easier said than done, I know. But try. The more you overcome your fear, the less fear cripples you. Be courageous. Courage is not the absence of fear. Courage is doing something in the face of fear. Don't let your insecurities stop you from trying.

With a mentor, or a team of mentors, you now have the makings of a wise council—an inner circle in your life that you allow to shape you, your values, and your decision-making. I believe that life is a team sport, not an individual sport.

I tell all my business partners to assemble a brain trust, an inner circle, or a board of directors. Think about the following scenario: Let's say that you are currently an intern at a local company, but you are not your average intern with average contacts. For the past few years, you've been working on befriending several influential and successful professionals in your community. You have coffee with a well-respected business owner on Mondays, attend a networking dinner with a top marketing consultant on Tuesdays, join a local investment club led by a seasoned investor on Wednesdays, participate in a Thursday evening fitness class with a successful entrepreneur, have breakfast with a career coach on Fridays, and volunteer at a community event with a retired executive on Saturdays.

Even though none of these people work directly in the industry you're interning in, what do you think your chances of succeeding in your career will be? I would guess around 100 percent. If you decide to continue working in your current field, you'll probably become one of the best professionals in your industry; you can't help but level up. By engaging in constant communication with other successful people, you will naturally internalize a great mindset and strategy. There's also a chance you'll think bigger and more strategically, and you might start your own business or take on leadership roles within your company. Eventually, you might become a key player in your industry. That's the power of a wise council. All ships rise with the tide.

I want you to ponder on the likelihood of growth for this intern. Like me, you're probably thinking this intern will go on to be a great businessperson; you'd start thinking like them and make decisions the way they would. We need to start with the people we know. Who are the people we admire and see frequently? Who are the people we can take for lunch and express our eagerness to level up? As Proverbs 27:17 (English Standard Version) says, "Iron sharpens iron, and one man sharpens another." I'm very fortunate to meet with my wise council in Orange County weekly.

We can't let our only mode of learning be trial and error. It's too exhausting. Your wise council members offer insights from their experiences, so you'll be compounding their efforts with your own. None of us is smarter than all of us. As an anonymous author says, "If you want to go fast, go alone. If you want to go far, go together." Don't go through life alone. Don't make big decisions on your own. Confide with people in your life whom you trust and respect. If you really want to be confident, partner your ambitions with a mentor. Real confidence comes from a collective brain trust with proven track records.

According to Tony Robbins, "Study people who have already achieved the result you're after. Success leaves clues." It doesn't matter what industry you're in or what job you're pursuing. There is someone who has achieved excellence in a capacity that you're hoping to emulate—whether in business, in marriage, parenting, and so on. It's your responsibility to find that person, pursue that person, and learn from that person. That person is the mentor you are looking for, whether you realize it or not. With that person in your corner, you have dramatically increased your probability of success. Instead of spending your own time and effort learning everything from scratch, you can start a few steps ahead by following the examples of mentors who have already walked the path you hope to follow.

How do you get the mentor's attention? Once again, I'll quote Julius Caesar: "Fortune favors the bold." Ask people if you can take them for breakfast, lunch, or dinner. Let them know why you'd like to meet with them. Many will feel purposeful giving back to a young, ambitious go-getter who reminds them of their younger selves. I think there are more people out there willing to lend a helping hand than most people realize.

Put yourself out there. Go places. Eagerly meet people. This approach put me at a dinner table with Steve Wozniak years ago. I was at the "right place at the right time" to make this dinner happen, and it was a moment with "the Woz" that I'll never forget. I was curious to hear firsthand how he and Steve Jobs built their little computer business into one of the world's most respected brands. We talked about little nerdy things such as where the company started—was it in the garage of Steve Jobs's parents, or was it in Steve Wozniak's bedroom? He was very kind, and he lit up talking about the good old days when he and Jobs had nothing—no money, no track record—and all that they had were dreams and vision. I've noticed that the supersuccessful love to reminisce about the good old days. It gives me some great perspective to not frantically run toward a destination but rather enjoy the process and journey.

Some people, like Steve, will give you their time; others will not. If you are lucky enough to meet up with them, here's my advice: give them a great return on their time. If the mentor gives you an hour of their time, prepare questions, take notes, and take action. Look to follow up once you've achieved something so they know their time had an impact. You're showing them that you bring a good return on investment of their time. Mentors will see that they gave you an hour, and you turned that into something very productive. They will be highly motivated to give you another hour. It is the student's job to motivate the teacher, not the other way around. By motivating the teacher, you will get more and more of their time, which arguably is the most valuable commodity that any of us possesses. In turn, you'll pay it forward and be a mentor for others. But for now, it is important for others to see that "the lights are on," and you're motivated to learn, seek mentorship, and eagerly grow. I wish I could say I have seen Steve Wozniak again since our dinner, but I have had the fortune of having a few follow-up conversations with him. Having a mentor or a wise council will help stretch us and help us grow into our potential.

The Impact of Self-Talk

When you try to do something outside the status quo, you'll find the naysayers, the haters, and you'll encounter self-doubt. I think most of us experience the "voice of discouragement" at various times in our lives. We have a feeling, or we hear a little voice that pops in our heads that tells us, "You can't do it. You're not good enough. What makes you think you deserve success? It's not worth it." You won't hear these things if you're just shooting for mediocrity. As David Goggins said, "You'll never meet a hater who is doing better than you." It's only the high achievers who have to deal with haters.

I'll try to answer these four questions:

- Where does this voice come from?
- Whose voice is it?
- Is it true?
- What can I do about this voice?

WHERE DOES THIS VOICE COME FROM?

Years ago, I had a new employee in my company who was very excited about the opportunity and showed a lot of promise. He asked if I could meet his parents because they had a lot of questions that he couldn't answer very well. I was confident in my business, my people, and where we were going, so I was honored to sit down with his parents. As I explained the opportunity to them, without their son in the room, they were impressed. I thought that the meeting was going great because they seemed to really buy into the vision and thought our model was amazing. I let them know that I enjoyed working with their son, and I thought that he had a lot of promise to do well with a little hard work, grit, and perseverance. However, they threw me a huge curveball. I'll never forget the conversation.

"You've only known our son for a few short weeks. We've known him his whole life. He starts things, gets really excited, and then he never follows through. We don't want him to be disappointed and letdown. He is speaking so positively about where he is going and what he is doing. We think he should work somewhere where he won't have such big aspirations so he won't be let down." I couldn't believe what I was hearing. It bothered me for weeks that followed; in fact, it even bothers me to this day.

As I've reflected, I think this is a common root in "the voice of discouragement." We may sabotage our futures by trying to avoid disappointment. Disappointment is the gap between expectations and reality. If you want to truly avoid disappointment, then don't set your expectations too high. If you have low expectations, you'll never experience disappointment. Our voices of discouragement—whether they are the voices of our parents, like in this example, or the voices of our teachers, or the voices of ourselves—are protective voices trying to shelter us from the disappointments that this world has to offer. After years of reflection, I'm convinced that this voice comes from a good place— from love. It's just trying to protect us. It's not hateful. It's not negative. It's just trying to derail us from disappointment, which can, in turn, cause many other problems such as a lack of confidence and discouragement.

Here's my advice: Thank the voice for the concern, love, and care; it is appreciated. But don't take the advice that avoiding disappointment offers. When you seek security, you never find it. When you seek opportunity, you find it *and* security. You might never leave the comfort of your home if security and safety are the goals. If you never leave your comfort zone, you never have the opportunity to grow. Aim high, and don't settle for something that is too low just to avoid disappointment. Avoid security and seek growth.

WHOSE VOICE IS IT?

As described in the example, our discouraging self-talk can come from family members early on in our lives. It can come from a teacher, a coach, a grandparent, a neighbor, and so on. It probably started with someone who was trying to protect you from disappointment. It can also come from our own failures and experiences. We fail at something one time, and then we tell ourselves that we're no good at it. We started believing this voice. Regardless of its origins, this limiting voice became our own voice. It became self-talk. It is important to recognize that this is our own voice. We need to own it and not be victims of our upbringing. No one can reprogram this voice but you. The good news is we *can* reprogram it with a little reflection and work, but it starts with owning it. When you own it, you also own the power to flip the script.

If you want to flip the script, it starts with recognizing that this doubtful talk exists, then taking ownership of it as your own. Then you need to make an effort to alter this voice. Speak new words into your talk; there is great power in the words we choose to speak. The biggest example I see as a father and as a Little League coach is young kids who say the words, "I can't." I always make a big deal about this language. I'll be firm and say, "Don't say that. It's not true. It's a lie. Here's a more accurate statement that I want you to start saying: 'It's difficult, but I *can* do it.' I can do it with enough persistence and practice. But never say, 'I can't.'" My kids know how sensitive I am to these words, but I believe there is power in our language. It is the self-talk that I want properly programmed for the spirit of growth.

IS THE VOICE TRUE?

The short answer is yes. There is merit behind the voice. We have enough experiences, failures, and disappointments to know that this voice is not make-believe. It came from someone and from somewhere. The parents who came into my office knew their son better than me. That was true. They saw him quit things. They saw him lose his enthusiasm as things started to become difficult. They knew the track record. I was so motivated to prove this set of parents wrong about their son. I gave this kid everything I had, took him under my wing, stacked his deck, everything. But in the end, the voice was stronger than my will and determination, and he ended up moving on, compromising his dreams for an easier job. Even if a voice has merit, it only holds power if we give it power. If we tell ourselves something over and over again, whether positive or negative, we can create self-fulfilling prophecies.

WHAT CAN I DO ABOUT THIS VOICE?

We need the right language. Some might think that going from "I can't" to "It's difficult, but I can" is too much of a stretch. You might try that talk temporarily, but in due time, you'll see enough losses to say to yourself, "I can't." May I offer a second talk track that might be helpful for you?

Try this on for size: "I will try, and I will do my best. At the very least, I will learn something." This is a very powerful script that can change the course of your destiny. Sometimes you win, sometimes you learn. The only time you lose is if you lose the lesson. Going into any task, job, or venture with this attitude is a game changer. It encourages you to stretch, challenge yourself, expand your comfort zone, and try new things. What do you have to lose? Time? Not true—you're learning. People pay big money and time to learn. Think of how much money and time people are willing to invest in a four-year degree. You really have nothing to lose. Try. Give it your best.

The following are the three types of self-talk:

- Negative self-talk
- Positive self-talk
- "Let me learn" self-talk

The latter two are the programs that I buy into. I believe the "Let me try" self-talk has more power than most people realize.

When motivation is lacking, that's when discipline takes over. Discipline will be your friend in Making Today Your Masterpiece. Fight through the temptation to quit or pack it in for the day and instead let the power of your discipline carry you through. Something very interesting happens.

Your confidence builds. You did something new, faced something you were afraid of, and found glimpses of hope and small victories. It keeps you coming back for more. It eventually becomes addictive—in a good way. You want to keep on trying. You gravitate toward difficult things, and you give your best effort. You start to develop a whole new track record in life: you try new things, you might struggle at first, and eventually, you start winning.

I first experienced this in door-to-door sales. I was afraid of people rejecting me. I was afraid of what others thought of me. I was afraid of not being accepted by friends or family. I met a girl, and for the first two months of dating, she thought I conducted "on-location advertising." I didn't have the confidence to tell her what I really did for a living. I remember being so ashamed when I finally told her that I sold coupons door to door on commission only. Surprisingly, she thought it was cool. She thought it was cool that I had the guts to do something that so many people wouldn't have the courage to do. Confidence bumped up. Skills improved. Income improved. Next thing you know, I'm telling everyone I knew that they should try sales based on my experience, self-improvement, and the absence of a glass ceiling on income. Confidence.

What comes first, the chicken or the egg? It can also be debated: What comes first, confidence or competence? I'm a believer that competence comes first, and then confidence will follow. Competence squashes negative self-talk. "Let me try and give my best" gives you a place to at least start. Persist. Keep going. Little wins come your way. Confidence builds. And eventually, you look at that negative self-talk and think to yourself, "I can't believe I used to be afraid. I can't believe I used to think that I couldn't." You can. You probably won't go from "I can't" to "I can" or "I will" overnight. The middle place is "I'll try and give my best." Progress is what's important, not perfection. If you're moving in the right direction, you are growing.

Whom Are You Serving?

Whom do we serve on a daily basis? For the most part, we serve ourselves. We focus on our tasks for the day, what we want to eat, and how to achieve our personal dreams. But I believe there is more to service than just meeting our own needs.

I've been studying and admiring Tom Brady for years. I don't know him personally, but I feel as though I do. I delighted in the *Tom vs Time* episodes on social media. I watched Tom fine-tune his craft over the years and loved observing him evolve into a premier quarterback in his forties. I believe most older people are secretly Tom Brady fans. Although they might not openly admit it because of their loyalty to their own teams, many older folks enjoy seeing "old guys rule." Tom's personal life has been interesting to observe—marriage, kids, hobbies, and then a humbling divorce. He seems humble, cool, and the ultimate guy you want on your team.

Yet with all of Tom's success, there was an interview I remember watching where Tom felt that there was something missing, some kind of void, and he couldn't identify what it was. This void might be the reason he is so obsessed with football and so great at it. He might be relentlessly trying to fill this void with being the GOAT. I'd love to have a conversation with Tom Brady about this. I believe that there is a God-sized void inside all of us that cannot be filled with success or self-indulgence. Maslow puts it another way in his "Hierarchy of Needs": we have our basic, physical needs at the bottom of the pyramid (food, water, shelter), and as our basic needs are met, we keep moving up the pyramid of needs. At the top of this pyramid, we have the needs of contribution and service. I believe, and it's only a hunch, that Tom could identify what is missing if he focuses on contribution and service and his spiritual growth. Something tells me that his chapters postretirement will have a lot of focus there, and Tom might very well find "what's missing."

When I read the book *Michael Jordan: The Life*, I could not put it down. It starts with Jordan's family background before his arrival. It goes into his early life as a child, including some of the conversations he had with his father and other family members. Some of these conversations can be credited to the origin of Michael's obsessive killer instincts that all of us observed on the basketball floor. It goes into his college and professional years. It goes into his business dealings with Nike. It goes into his baseball experiences. It goes into his days with the Wizards. MJ was one of the most influential people on the planet. The world was obsessed with him. When he came out of retirement to play basketball again, companies such as Hanes and Wheaties experienced massive gains in the market. Everyone wanted a piece of Michael Jordan. He was an amazing example of success for the world to watch.

The last couple of chapters shocked and challenged me, and probably many readers, to look at a different side of MJ. Michael was lucky enough to be one of the most influential people on the planet. Think of how many organizations around the world would have loved to have him as a spokesperson or endorser. What cause could Michael Jordan get behind and do his part to change the world? That's a pretty amazing place to be for any individual. What was the cause that Michael got behind? According to the book, he got behind the cause of *self* for the most part. I don't know what MJ does with his time; all I know is the picture that the media paints:

gambling, golf, girls, cigars, self-pleasure. There's nothing this guy could not have. I'm not a Jordan hater or condemning MJ by any means. He is still the GOAT in basketball and arguably the GOAT of GOATS. I'm just saying this book challenged me to look at MJ's life and opportunities from a different lens.

The last couple of chapters of the book discussed how this icon, one of the most influential people on the planet, didn't use his celebrity status to serve or make the world a better place. Of course, MJ has made considerable donations to worthy causes, but he was never the spokesperson behind any global movements. This is where I go back to Tom Brady's interview about "something missing." If we are lucky enough to have the resources the way these two megastars have, we can try our best to fill our inner void. Fill it with winning. Fill it with being the best in the world. Fill it with pleasure. Fill it with recognition and success. But unfortunately, we will find ourselves filling it with something that simply will not satisfy—unless we have a higher calling or a higher purpose to help others. I am convinced of this. I think I was around twelve years old when I realized it felt better to give a gift to someone at Christmas than it was to receive a gift. We have spiritual needs that deserve our attention and focus. However you define your spiritual being, you have a deep need to serve and contribute to others.

One last celebrity example to drive the question, Whom are you serving? I remember watching the news the night Princess Diana was in a car accident in France. I stayed up to watch how this would unfold. The headlines initially read, "Princess Diana injured in a serious car accident." Eventually, the media updated the headlines to "Princess Diana is pronounced dead." Wow. I was shocked, and the world was just as shocked as I was. A few days later, Princess Diana's funeral was held. As the hearse drove through the streets of England, people came out and pelted the vehicle with flowers. The driver had to eventually get out and remove these flowers from the windshield because he could not see. The people of England really loved her. Then I found out that her funeral was observed by two billion people around the planet. That was approximately one-third of the entire planet watching this woman's funeral.

Why was the world so obsessed with Princess Diana? Obviously, there is the stardom associated with just being royalty and, of course, the drama of going through a divorce and so on. But one-third of the planet? There must be more. Of course, there's more. We saw a woman who had it all—just like Michael Jordan, Tom Brady, or any other high-end celebrities. She possessed power, she was rich, and she challenged the old-school traditions of the monarchy. But the thing we *loved* about Princess Diana was that she dedicated her life to people in need. She spent time in third-world countries, connecting to people in poverty. She was obsessed with the removal of all land mines around the world that caused so much harm to people. This princess stepped out of her castle and spent her life serving people in need. We admired that. We fell in love with her.

I'm not saying that we need to give all our time and resources away to charity. I don't think there's anything wrong with owning a nice home, a nice car, a nice watch, and so on. I don't think there's anything wrong with spoiling yourself and your loved ones with an awesome vacation. What I am saying is that serving *you* can't be your only service. It's not enough for the Grow Right principles. The more reasons you have to work hard and serve others, the more incentive and motivation you'll have to improve yourself and make a difference in the lives of others.

Let's say you and I had to bet on which of two different people would be more successful. Both have the same credentials, skill sets, and backgrounds. Person A has one reason to be successful: to make themselves happy. Person B has one hundred reasons to be successful: primarily to make others happy. If Person B has people connected to several of these one hundred reasons, I would bet on Person B. The person with one hundred reasons to be successful has more people to serve, more incentive, and more motivation. This gives them a greater drive to improve and grow.

If we want to be joyful and live purpose-driven lives, then we need to look for organizations and people outside ourselves to contribute. This will be the rocket fuel that allows us to grow. I think if we really play our lives to the best of our abilities, life will be broken up into three phases: Learn, Earn, and Return.

- Learn: Be a student, be a sponge, study and master your craft.
- Earn: The top 5 percent of people in any industry make great money. Be a performer and earn.
- Return: Plan on giving it all away. Don't be a reservoir with your money; be a river. Be committed to a life of service.

Wear Your Jersey Well

I wonder how many LeBron James or Lionel Messi jerseys are sold each year. There are millions of people around the world that like to sport the jerseys of their favorite athletes. Personally, I'll wear a team jersey with the logo on the front, but I refuse to have someone's name on my back. My back is reserved for one name and one name only: "Hepp." I don't want to wear someone else's jersey; that's not whom I represent.

When Michael Jordan returned from his first retirement, he didn't want to wear #23 because his father was no longer around to watch him play. This was a new beginning for Michael, and #45 was his first number when he played in high school. After losing to the Magic in game 1 of the playoffs, Michael abandoned the #45 jersey and went back to #23, returning to his GOAT jersey. Some think that the NBA should retire the number 23 because no one will wear that jersey as well as Michael Jordan did.

I challenge everyone to wear their jerseys well. Whether you know it, you're walking around every day with your family jersey on. You're leaving a legacy for all people who follow after you. What do you want that legacy to look like? By reflecting on your family reputation, your last name, it might give you one more reason to Grow. Grow Right. Grow Right Now.

Lucky for me, my second cousin (Michael Hepp) had the time

and curiosity to research our ancestry. He flew to Germany to find out the history of our family. He ended up tracing our family back to the 1400's and found our family moving throughout Europe in pursuit of finding better opportunities for their offspring. Michael's book filled with "Heppisodes" left a mark on me for two reasons.

First, it is interesting to see that a part of my motivation is really a part of my DNA. I, too, am highly motivated to help my offspring live better lives than the life I grew up with. It's in my blood. As my family left the comforts of Germany for Hungary and other European areas, I left the comforts of small-town Canada to pursue success in the big cities of the United States.

Second, the book is filled with a ton of hardship and adversity. It has many details about our family from the 1850s to the present, including the migration from Germany to Ellis Island in pursuit of the American dream—like so many other Europeans. My family went through immense hardship to provide opportunity for me and the other Hepps who would follow. They left family behind knowing that they'd never see them again. They didn't speak the common language in America. They worked in factories in New York, where they would clock in sixty-to-eighty-hour workweeks in conditions that resemble sweatshops today. My great-great-grandfather worked in a cotton factory and, in his later years, had to undergo surgery to remove a wad of cotton which had collected in his stomach from inhaling and swallowing cotton fibers day after day. Eventually, the Hepps took advantage of the free land in Canada that the government offered; otherwise, I might have ended up being a New Yorker.

All of us have a history, and it might be a good idea to get as much of the history as you can from your elderly family who's still alive. Chances are, you don't have a great-uncle who documented your family's journey in a book. On one of my last visits with my father-in-law, I was intrigued to know his family's history, telling him that my children will probably want to know. At the very least, the medical field tells us that family history has a lot to do with our predisposition and how our DNA can predict heart issues, cancer, hair loss, and so on. My father-in-law loved the conversation and appreciated my eagerness to learn, especially about those "good old days."

As you learn about your history, you might be motivated to either keep the family reputation thriving or put the family name on a different trajectory. Likely, your family went through some very difficult times, and your ancestors probably yearned for their offspring to have it better than they had it. What an insult it would be to wear our family jerseys untucked and lazily—apathetic and indifferent to their struggle for family survival. Wear your jersey with pride and respect. Wear it with enthusiasm to make the next generation better than the previous. There will be some kind of offspring in your lineage, whether direct (your own children) or indirect (nephews, nieces, distant cousins, and so on). If there are trends that you're not proud of, make the decision to break the cycle and start a new trend. Maybe others in the family didn't think much of the jerseys they were wearing. From this day forward, what are the characteristics you want for your family members? What values from your ancestry should be continued and valued? What new values would you want to include under your last name? What will your family be known for? Stand for those values. Live for those values.

I come from a lineage of tough Germans who work very hard to provide better lives for the next generation, and I plan on keeping that reputation by wearing my jersey well. I want my children to have better lives than me, and I hope they pass this mindset along to their children.

The Domino Phenomenon

It is possible to become paralyzed with a lack of motivation and action because there are just too many areas in one's life that need improvement. I have witnessed "the Domino Phenomenon" play out too many times in too many people's lives. Here's an example of how this phenomenon works: Bob is arguing with his girlfriend. They are up late at night and have disagreements. As a result, Bob is tired the next day, with his thoughts consumed by the argument. Bob's work is now affected by his fatigue and lack of focus. Bob gains five pounds because he's not eating right, nor does he have the motivation to go to the gym right now. Bob is short in his conversations with everyone, and everyone notices he's irritable. Bob is basically "losing" in many areas of his life because he allowed one of his life's compartments—in this case, the girlfriend compartment—to negatively influence other compartments of his life, such as health compartment, relationships with others compartment, and so on. I'm sure we have all experienced this or witnessed this with others. One thing leads to another, and next thing you know, there's a chain reaction, and now our lives overall just suck. As a result of life's challenges, we might find ourselves "starting over" in multiple areas of our lives, such as after a breakup or losing a job, and completely resetting everything.

The way to avoid this is to compartmentalize. If the girlfriend compartment is suffering, then that means we need to make sure other compartments in our lives are thriving so we don't lose complete confidence and become train wrecks. We *must* protect our confidence. We will all be in a better place dealing with issues if we are mentally healthy and feeling good about ourselves. In Bob's example, his self-esteem is going downhill in all areas. If Bob were succeeding in other compartments of his life, he would be in a much better place to find solutions with this girlfriend.

I suggest having basic categories in life that you can take inventory of and use to evaluate yourself. The goal is to not let one category spill into the other. They should be independent. This works both ways. Even if I feel like I'm doing well in one compartment, I don't let that confidence spill into another compartment and become overconfident. Pride always comes before the fall. Keep compartments independent. This will help you maintain your confidence while still growing in all areas of your life.

Here are a few basic categories:

- Physical health
- Mental health
- Spiritual health
- Relationship with a significant other
- Family relationships
- Friends
- Finances
- Career

We could also break each category into subcategories. I'll give you an example that happens to me a lot. Regarding the category of physical health, I get sports injuries from time to time. When I'm injured and can't go to the gym, I won't be able to achieve my physical health goals; I won't be able to push myself on the treadmill the way I like to. Since I won't achieve my calorie-burning (output) goals this week, I better make up for it by improving my calorie intake. In other words, this week I need to eat less and intake fewer calories because I can't get to the gym. If I don't take action in response to this curveball, I could potentially add on extra pounds and find myself losing in the compartment of physical health. I need the little wins, and I must be willing to pivot when things come up. Because I adjusted in my subcategory of physical health and weight, I was able to maintain my confidence even though I couldn't exercise as I normally do. In this way, I was still "growing right."

I have found that if there are opportunities to experience "double wins"—winning in multiple categories while doing the same task—you should seize these opportunities to grow your confidence and cement great habits. I love these double wins. Here's an example: I find myself going to the gym more often because I can rip through books on Audible and explore fascinating podcasts. The more I yearn for great mental growth, the more I yearn to go to the gym. The gym is the sidekick and companion to the mental learning that I love so much. This is a great double win. I'm winning in the mental health category and winning, as a by-product, in the physical health category.

Here's a triple-win example that I love: Take a group of coworkers and family members to a baseball game. You'll be winning in the family compartment by spending quality time with loved ones, strengthening work relationships by developing closer bonds with coworkers, and fulfilling your need for the entertainment compartment. Throw some icing on the cake with a thrilling game where the home team wins a nail-biter. You'll walk out of a ball game feeling like a champion. Look for the wins. Look for the confidence build. Categorize your life in a way that you don't let losses affect other important areas of your life. Avoid chain reactions. Avoid the "Domino Phenomenon."

The Diamond Rule

I wanted to know everything about diamonds before proposing to JoAnne. It was shocking how expensive these little rocks were, so I wanted to make sure I was getting the best value and the best ring for my soon-to-be bride. I was referred to a diamond wholesaler in downtown Los Angeles. This guy helped many of my friends purchase diamonds for their brides, and he gave me an education. I learned about the four C's: cut, color, clarity, and carat. The combination of these four factors will determine the value of the diamond. I still remember the exact dimensions of JoAnne's engagement ring.

Over the years I've developed a little system and mantra when dealing with people, and I look for evaluation and self-improvement in these areas. I call it "the Diamond Rule" because it has the four C's, just like a diamond.

The Diamond Rule:

- Never criticize
- Never condemn
- Never compare
- Never complain

If you've read *How to Win Friends and Influence People,* by Dale Carnegie, you'll recognize three of these in the book (never criticize, condemn, or complain). I wanted to add a fourth one (never compare). It's simple to think of a diamond and the four C's. In my mind, it's a blueprint for healthy interactions with people. If we grow in these "Diamond Rule" areas, I believe our relationships will be better and stronger. I have some thoughts on criticism, condemning, comparing, and complaining that I believe are noteworthy.

NEVER CRITICIZE

Criticizing is a great way to alienate people and shatter a person's confidence. Unless someone is seeking feedback, criticism should not be offered, as we want to be a force for good in the lives of others. We won't experience positive growth if we make others feel less confident because of our interactions. I mentioned in "Find a Mentor" that the problem with most of us is that we'd rather be ruined by praise than saved by criticism. Seeking criticism is different from *offering* criticism. If a person isn't looking for it, then I'm not looking to offer it. I take this rule very seriously. When it comes to praising, I'm all about it. In fact, I've only posted five-star reviews on Yelp and Google. That doesn't mean that everywhere I go, I receive a five-star experience. I only publicly call out the five-star reviews. If I have a bad experience, I don't believe the web is the best platform to air out my dissatisfaction. I don't want to be an online complainer or, as Steve Harvey calls them, "Thumb Gangsters." If my experience is less than five stars, I won't post anything. I don't want to hurt an establishment. People's livelihoods are on the line. If I have a one-, two-, or three-star kind of experience, I'll ask to speak to someone there. I'll let a boss or manager know what happened, not to complain and get something for free but to give them the chance to help the employees and train the staff. It's always been a reasonable conversation and welcomed. I ask myself, "Am I a lifter or a leaner? Do I pick people up, or do I bring them down? How do people feel around me? How do they feel about themselves? How do they feel about me?" If you're a person who offers others unsolicited criticism, there's a good chance you're not exactly winning in the "lifting department." Make others feel good. Catch people doing things right. Offer people smiles and compliments. And never criticize.

NEVER CONDEMN

Condemning is judging with complete disapproval. We tend to judge other people by their actions, and we tend to judge ourselves by our intentions. It's quite the double standard.

I found myself as a nitpicker and a perfectionist in my early years of owning my business. My intentions were good—I was tough on people because I cared and wanted to see them grow. I thought tough love was something that everyone would eventually appreciate, as I have appreciated tough coaches and bosses over the years. But that's not how it shook out for many. I think many people felt condemned when I pushed them to a mark that was simply too high for them. I think, as I look back, that people don't really remember the things that you did or the things that you said. People remember how they felt around you. And when people don't feel good about themselves when they are around you, they simply won't want to be around you. I lost focus on the bigger picture when it came to developing those around me by not being sensitive to how people felt. I was too tough, too condemning. I suggest taking this lesson to heart; otherwise, we risk paying the price of severed relationships.

NEVER COMPARE

In Jordan Peterson's book *12 Rules for Life*, one of his rules is this: "Compare yourself to who you were yesterday, not to who someone else is today." I love that. It has the essence of the Grow Right principle in it (compare yourself with you) and the age-old wisdom of not comparing yourself with others. Comparing yourself with others is so unhealthy. As Theodore Roosevelt said, "Comparison is the thief of joy." It creates envy and jealousy, and these two traits expose the ugly side of us very quickly. We need to be thankful for our lives, our situations, and the shoes we walk in. One of the life lessons my father taught me in high school is, "I complained that I had no shoes until I saw a man that had no feet." There should be no one else on the planet that we'd like to trade shoes with. No one. You are unique, and you were made with purpose. Envy no one else. There will always be someone else richer, better looking, with a better body, a better everything. Don't seek greener grass on the other side of the fence. The greenest grass is the grass that you water. It's possible to learn this lesson the hard way—being discontent and unhappy for extended periods. I believe that it's okay to want more for yourself and your family, but not at the expense of envy in the heart. Wanting what someone else has is a recipe for dissatisfaction of the soul and constant and never-ending unhappiness.

NEVER COMPLAIN

If you're a child growing up in my home, then you would know that I don't tolerate complaining. Maybe my lack of tolerance comes from my high school days when my old basketball coach, Kevin Grieman, would yell at us when we'd complain, "Would you like some cheese to go with your whine?"

I tell my kids that complaining is a sign of being spoiled. Spoiled people complain. I am completely embarrassed about the things that I used to complain about (and still do from time to time). It's embarrassing because when I really think about it and reflect, I'm complaining because I'm a spoiled brat. I'll complain about the traffic in LA—easy one to complain about. But then I stopped and thought. I had an opportunity to serve an Operation Smile medical trip in San Cristobal, Mexico, where families traveled for days on donkeys to help their child get an operation for a cleft lip. They could only wish to be driving in a car and dealing with LA traffic or wish for a life in a first-world nation for that matter.

Years ago, as a door-to-door salesman, I was having a bad day. I had many bad days, but this day was extra bad. It was raining, I was hungry, and I had some squabbles with my girlfriend the night before. I was struggling with compartmentalizing my problems. I felt so sorry for myself. Woe is me. Hours went by without making a sale. Around six in the evening, a young girl in a wheelchair answered the door. She was vibrant and excited to see me, unlike everyone else in the neighborhood. She invited me into her home because I looked cold. She also said I looked hungry and asked me if I'd like some hot chocolate. She wheeled away and brought me back a nice, hot drink. Then she asked me what I was doing. I unenthusiastically told her about the promotion I was selling, expecting her to say no like everyone else did. She said, "That sounds great. Can I buy one?"

I almost gagged on my drink. "Can you buy one? Uh, yeah." I was surprised, considering I never met a person until that time who asked if they could buy my promotion.

After making the transaction and drinking my hot chocolate, I thanked the young lady and wished her well. As I walked down the driveway, my first thought was, "Man, that was the easiest sale I've ever made." My second thought was, "Man, am I ever a jerk. This girl has a fraction of the opportunities in life than I have, and she has a positive, winning attitude, and I'm out here moping around feeling sorry for myself. She probably wishes that she had the opportunity to walk in the rain while I'm out here complaining about it."

Complaining is a sign that you're spoiled. Easy solution to avoid complaining: Start losing things. If you're not careful, complaining will lead to a plethora of losses—relationally and physically. Value the things you value. The remedy for complaining and envy is gratitude. Gratitude for the greenest grass growing right underneath your feet. Look to improve in the Diamond Rule, and your relationships and your inner peace will improve drastically.

Willing to Experiment

I have done some really stupid and embarrassing things over the course of my life. My wife says it's because I'm Canadian, and I probably watched too much Bob and Doug McKenzie growing up.

This next story is hard for me to write. It's something I can't believe that I had such poor character to actually do, but this story will emphasize a major point that I want to get across in this chapter.

Here goes.

I wasn't doing well as a rookie owner in business. I didn't know how to recruit people, and I was even worse at training these few new recruits to become great salespeople. I was failing in business, and I was near the end of the entrepreneurial road. I needed help. I needed advice.

Someone who had a lot of experience and was doing well in his business asked me if I had ever fired anyone publicly in a morning meeting. Of course, I had not. He advised me that I should do it, and this would shake things up in my office. I had a difficult time convincing myself this was the right thing to do, but I was desperate and willing to try just about anything.

I had a rep who wasn't doing very well, and it was just a matter of time until we were going to part ways; I was sure that he was on the verge of quitting sometime soon; the writing was on the wall. He seemed like the guy I should "stretch my comfort zone" with.

After giving praise to the top producer of the day in a morning meeting, I said, "We have another guy I want to draw attention to." Everyone was confused because they all knew the top producer was just recognized. There was no one else who beat out the top producer.

"This next guy is late often. He constantly underperforms in the field. And he isn't adding much value to the team." I called his name and then said, "Please turn in your badge. We won't be working together any longer."

My face was red with embarrassment. His face was red with embarrassment. Everyone in the office was in disbelief that this just happened. I tried my best to continue the meeting after that awkward display of humiliation and wrapped things up quickly. After everyone left to go to the field, I immediately called him to apologize.

"I am so sorry. You didn't deserve that. Please accept my apology."

"No, Jaime, I'm sorry. You were right. I have been a bad example, and I'm sorry."

"No, listen, regardless of how you performed, no one should be treated that way."

We exchanged many apologies back and forth. Lucky for me, he was willing to forgive me. I also apologized to my entire office for my poor character and lack of leadership. My team appreciated the apology, and they made it clear that what I did was anything but motivating.

I learned a couple of things through that experience.

The first lesson was obvious—don't ever, *ever* treat someone like that. Public humiliation is the opposite of leadership. It's immature, insensitive, disrespectful, and unloving. I promised myself that I would never do that again. It's kind of crazy to write this down after the last chapter about never criticizing, condemning, comparing, or complaining. The same person (me) who fired someone publicly is now the same person (me) who won't write anything less than a five-star review online. I think becoming a person of character is a result of the Grow Right principle.

I like the advice of "shake things up" in the office, just not exactly what my old, experienced friend had in mind.

Try things such as the following:

- If someone has a rough sales day and feels awful about the result, praise them for trying and toughing it out. It's not the yeses that make us successful; it's how we handle the noes.
- If someone has a very high sales day and everyone in the office is high-fiving and praising the person, maybe you can challenge the person, and let them know that you want to see *that* kind of jubilant smile and attitude on a low-performing day.
- If someone is in a slump and can't seem to get out of it, give them a homework assignment to send an email outlining why they still want to work here. Articulate the why. The person might think it through and decide they don't want to work here. The person might think it through and realize they want to grow and succeed here, and maybe this is the catalyst for the necessary changes. I've seen people reevaluate their effort and turn things around after really thinking through the why.
- If the office had a bad day collectively, instead of being upset as everyone might expect you to be, come in singing "Zip-a-Dee-Doo-Dah," and life is awesome. Completely unexpected.

The list goes on and on. There are countless scenarios when dealing with people. Only through experimentation and evaluation can we fine-tune our best coaching skills. Experiment with integrity and a concern for others.

The second lesson I learned from the public firing was that, man, was I willing to stretch my comfort zone. I was willing to try things to the extreme. There is no manual for the business I was running. I needed to learn to lead people, learn to push myself and others, and experiment. Now the asterisk is to experiment with integrity and class, but experiment nonetheless. Growth happens at the outskirts of your comfort zone.

I read Phil Jackson's book *Sacred Hoops*. Of course, I knew that Phil was a player himself, and of course, I knew him as the eleven-time championship coach. What I found fascinating in the book was what took place between the time he was a player and the time he took on his coaching job with the Chicago Bulls. What was Phil doing in that "undocumented time" of his life that the public didn't witness?

Phil wanted to coach basketball and took on a coaching job in Puerto Rico for five years. To say it was a bush league is an understatement. Some of the examples of this bush league were they played in outdoor arenas, there was an incident of a fan shooting a referee during a game, there were tarantulas in the dressing rooms, and so on. Not exactly his dream job. But it's where Phil needed to start. It's where Phil had his chance to experiment with his players. How do you develop your players? How do you push your players? How do you treat them? Do you treat them the same? Do you treat them differently? What do you do with the players with big egos? What do you do with your players who are always in the gym? What do you do with the players who have troubled lives outside the game? The list is never ending. How is anyone supposed to know the answers to these questions?

We need experience. With reflection, we will get the evaluated experience that later turns into insight and wisdom. By the time Phil went to Chicago for his coaching assignment, he was prepared.

He knew what to do with Michael Jordan, and he knew how to treat the superstar of the team. He knew how to deal with Pippen, BJ, Grant, and the list goes on. He knew how to deal with a wild card such as Dennis Rodman. He knew this because he had significant hours under his belt coaching, and he failed many times over and over. It could be said he knew what not to do more than he knew what to do.

If you try to avoid failure, you're just asking to delay failure. Fail fast. Fail often. Course correct. Improve. Stretch your comfort zone. We must be willing to experiment and try new things. Remember this: we never lose as long as we never lose the lesson.

Expect the Worst and Hope for the Best

As stated earlier, I started my career as a commission-only, door-to-door salesperson. I didn't have a wealthy family to call for backup in the event that I couldn't pay my bills. I was on my own and independent, and I couldn't be wasteful or extravagant with my finances.

This forced me to be frugal. I couldn't afford any mismanagement of my money in case I got into a sales slump, so I always looked for ways of keeping my expenses very low. Many times I had multiple roommates. There was a time fifteen of us lived in a three-bedroom townhome. Sure, the living conditions were tight, but everyone's rent was $200 per month. We didn't complain. We found ways of making the environment as hospitable as possible, such as labeling the cupboards and refrigerator for individual and shared food items. We had a bathroom schedule taped to the wall. For those who liked to sleep in, they paid the price with a quick, cold shower in the mornings. These were the humble beginnings of my career. It's been said that it's not a person's lack of resources that prevents someone from success; rather, it's a lack of resourcefulness. Resourcefulness was our middle name. We made every penny count.

As time went on, I accumulated some savings, and my resources started to add up. However, the mentality of frugality never left. I always wanted to be prepared for the worst-case scenarios while maintaining hope and optimism for the best outcome. One day, as I was driving through Los Angeles with JoAnne (while we were still dating), I pointed to an area near the freeway and exclaimed, "If I'm ever homeless, that's exactly where I'm going to live. That's the perfect spot." I wasn't really thinking much about her reaction. Instead, I was thinking that I discovered the jackpot of locations for worst-case scenarios. It was only slightly visible from the freeway, difficult to access because of fencing and a busy street nearby, and I'm pretty sure that if I had a little barbecue, the smoke wouldn't be visible. JoAnne asked me if there was anything that she should know. I started laughing, as it hadn't occurred to me until that moment how far I'd come since the humble beginnings of my business.

I'm happy to report that the worst-case scenario never happened and that JoAnne still decided to marry me, even though I gave her a pretty solid red flag with my search for the perfect place to reside in the event of homelessness. I do think, however, that this is a very healthy mindset. When you prepare for the worst, you will never be blindsided or completely disappointed. Remember, disappointment is the gap between expectations and reality. In all probability, you will probably never experience the worst-case scenario. It's just not likely. Couple this mental preparation with an optimistic lens for the future—be hopeful. You'll have the shield of expecting the worst to protect you, and you'll have the weaponry of a great attitude and optimism to achieve greatness. Expect the worst and hope for the best.

Stuck behind the Pace Car

I worked hard over the years to eradicate any ounce of a victim mindset that might have been holding me back. It served me no good to think that I was a victim, even in situations where most people would have concluded that I was wronged.

A victim mindset—believing that we have been wronged—opens the door for excuses and alibis to reside in our minds. Once we allow excuse making into the fabric of our character, we give other people and circumstances the power to shape our destiny. We are never products of our circumstances; rather, we are products of our decisions. I believe this to be true.

To help build a culture of "No Excuses" in my business, I periodically ran an excuse contest. I gave the entire team (sales reps, office personnel, and management) one week to come up with the best excuse for any situation they encountered for the week—whether it be for poor performance, tardiness, or anything that led to the opposite result that was intended. The winner received a $100 cash bonus, and it would be fun for everyone. As the week rolled along, the team thought about the potential excuses they could make when things didn't go their way. I believe this exercise cemented the mindset of accountability, as they were consciously hunting for opportunities to make excuses. It made us all realize that we could come up with excuses for just about anything. But when things went well, we would never make excuses; we would like to take the credit for a job well done. Take the credit; pass the blame.

We judged the winner based on applause and laughter as everyone took a turn to share their best excuse. One of our contest winners was a sales rep who came in late one day. It happened to be the week of the Grand Prix in Long Beach. He arrived late to work because he had been stuck in traffic, right around the track area. Logically, he pondered, "I must be stuck behind the pace car." He was a very good storyteller, and he brought a lot of emotion, frustration, and fun to his testimony. We broke out laughing and crowned our newest excuse champion.

This periodic exercise of "excuse contests" was good for our culture, but I believed there was more that I could do. I felt that I needed to improve my ability to hold other people accountable. I asked myself, "Are there more effective ways that I can hold people accountable to high standards in productive ways without damaging the relationships?" That's a pretty good question for anyone in a leadership position. I came up with a list of five people I wanted to call and learn from. These people had great organizations, and they led very talented people. I began making my calls.

The first four people gave me great advice and tips on how to get the best out of others while building confidence in their people during crucial conversations. I appreciated their wisdom as they shared valuable golden nuggets with me. The fifth person, however, changed my paradigm. I saved the best for last, as this person was the most successful, in my opinion, at holding others to a high standard.

I outlined my intent for the call, and I shared my observations of his team. His people never seemed to make excuses regardless of the challenging situations I'd seen them in. The team seemed to always get the job done regardless of the circumstances. He listened to me intently, and he paused, as he was not quick to give me an impulsive answer. After a period, he told me that he didn't think he was very good at holding others accountable, and maybe I should consider talking to someone else who was better in this field. I was confused. "You don't believe that you're good at holding people accountable? I think you're great in this area. I must be missing something."

He replied, "I think I'm lucky. First of all, I only hire self-accountable people, so I don't have to hold them accountable. If anything, they're too tough on themselves and hold themselves to very high standards. Second, I was lucky with my kids. They, too, are highly self-accountable, and I didn't have to push them either. They did their homework, they received good grades, and they work hard at their jobs. So I don't think I have much practice in the area of holding others accountable. I just know how to discipline myself and hold myself accountable. This is why I think you might want to call around and get some better advice."

That was all I needed to hear. I found what I was looking for. One of the characteristics of growing right is the ability to be self-disciplined and self-accountable. Listening to my friend humbly share his thoughts highlighted a very important principle: self-accountability can be contagious. When you model self-mastery, others, such as your teammates, your children, and so on, will potentially reflect this mindset.

I tell my children, "You can choose to be self-disciplined, or you can choose to let others discipline you. Either way, you can't escape discipline." On an extreme level, as an example, if you cannot hold yourself accountable to the laws and rules of this country, we have a judicial system that will hold you accountable. Growing right embodies self-discipline and self-control.

I've come across many great quotes over the years on the topics of excuses, accountability, and eliminating victimhood. These quotes own a small piece of my memory bank. They have aided me on my journey of self-accountability and growth. I hope these quotes help you destroy the enemy of excuse making. As you read each quote, ponder the power of these truths, and try adding them to your character repertoire.

- "I attribute my success to this: I never gave or took any excuse."—Florence Nightingale
- "I never knew a man who was good at making excuses who was good at anything else."—Benjamin Franklin
- "If you can't be a good example, then you'll just have to be a horrible warning."—Catherine Aird
- "It is easier to go from failure to success than it is to go from excuses to success."—John Maxwell
- "An excuse is a skin of a reason stuffed with a lie."—Billy Sunday
- "No one can make you feel inferior without your consent."—Eleanor Roosevelt
- "Nobody can hurt me without my permission."—Mahatma Gandhi
- "Don't tell me how rocky the sea is; just bring the damn ship in."—Anonymous
- "I am not concerned that you have fallen; I am concerned that you arise."—Abraham Lincoln
- "You can do the right thing, or you can do the easy thing."—Anonymous
- "For every person that climbs the ladder of success, there are dozens waiting for the elevator."—Anonymous
- "IF—and this is the greatest of them all—I had the courage to see myself as I really am, I would find out what is wrong with me, and correct it, then I might have a chance to profit by my mistakes and learn something from the experience of others. For I know that there is something wrong with me, or I would now be where I would have been if I had spent more time analyzing my weaknesses, and less time building alibis to cover them."—Napoleon Hill

Mr. Learn-It-All

No one likes Mr. Know-It-All. He is arrogant and tough to be around. He thinks he's so smart and has all the right answers. He's quick to offer advice and typically likes hearing the sound of his own voice. Mr. Know-It-All doesn't get invited to collaboration meetings much.

But do you know Mr. Learn-It-All? Mr. Learn-It-All is a completely different human being. He is curious and wants to know what works, how it works, and why it works. He asks questions with the intent to listen, to feel, and to implement new things.

As a young adult, I think I was guilty of being a Mr. Know-It-All. I believed that I knew how the world worked; I had the answers. Funny, the older I get, the "less intelligent" I feel. The more experiences I'm exposed to and the more self-aware I become, the more I realize that I don't know. "Mr. Learn-It-All" wants more information, wisdom, and growth. His mindset is essential to Grow Right.

Many years ago I crossed paths with a young Patrick Bet-David. We were both young men in our twenties trying to make it in life and in business, and we enjoyed spending time with each other. We made it a habit to meet up for dinners at one of our favorite restaurants in Los Angeles—Bamboo. We still talk about the *sopa de vegetable* at Bamboo. We shared our goals, desires, visions, and challenges in business. On many occasions we finished our evenings (past midnight) sitting in a parked car across the street from luxury car dealerships, cementing our dream cars in our minds.

Pat had (and to this day still has) an insatiable appetite to learn. He wants to know how people think, what drives them, and how they look at the world. I love my dinners and conversations with Pat. He inspires me to learn, to keep asking curious questions, and to do something about my personal growth.

During our dinners, we often recommend books for each other. On many occasions, Pat would go the extra mile. He didn't just recommend the books. Surprisingly, he bought the books, wrote great messages inside the books, and then shipped them off in the mail for me. If we talked about history and leadership, for example, *Lincoln on Leadership* would arrive at my door. He pushed me to be aggressive with my self-education. He was always very thoughtful and a masterful learner. I have many books in my personal library from this hungry man. It's no surprise to me that Pat is as successful as he is. He has many great attributes, and one of those shining characteristics is his eagerness to "learn it all."

I have found that the learn-it-alls in this world don't lack self-esteem. The smartest and most successful people I know ask more questions than give answers. I started observing this at conferences and functions where our group of top leaders, managers, recruiters, and owners would gather. I observed that the two people in the industry who made the most money spent their time asking questions. In my mind, it seemed like they already knew the answers to these questions—or at least they were the most qualified individuals to answer these thoughtful questions. Why were they so curious? Why were they always engaging with questions?

Then I observed some of the people who struggled in business seemed to do a lot of talking. Not asking questions, just talking. They lacked the "hungry student mentality," and I noticed that many opportunities were missed for these people being around the superstars.

I think we all start off as curious students. As a parent I'm met with questions that I haven't asked myself in years. I love the eagerness to learn and grow. I think these struggling people in business weren't always talking. At some point they were asking questions, learning, and growing. What happened? What changed?

This might not be the case every time, but I think what happens is that people start buying into their own press when praise and success start happening. Others recognize the success and offer sincere compliments as they witness their peers, colleagues, children, and others grow and succeed. It's difficult to keep up with the image of success if people see you asking questions and not having all the answers. I certainly noticed this in my life. I'd find myself catching a wave of success and gaining some great positive momentum, and then all of a sudden, I was on the downturn, and I didn't even notice. Time kept ticking, and next thing you know, I was in a full slump, losing confidence with every step, it seemed. Through enough ups and downs, I noticed that I consistently stopped growing when momentum was positive. I stopped asking questions. I thought I either knew what I was doing or I thought that I didn't want to look weak. It's pretty easy to ask questions when you're sucking—that seems like a natural thing to do. Asking questions when you're kicking butt seems counterintuitive; however, that is the necessary ingredient to avoid the unnecessary downturns.

Looking back over history, it would have made a lot more sense to have gravitated to others who had lived longer and had gone through the challenges that I hadn't anticipated yet. I could have asked the million-dollar question: "Based on where I'm at now, what roadblocks and challenges should I anticipate, and how can I best prepare for these challenges?" Asking this question could have helped me avoid pain, and it would have led to a Mr. Learn-It-All marathon of questions to keep me in the "growing zone." In my opinion the number-one indicator of intelligence is curiosity. It will serve us well in our adult lives if we can get back to our childhood curiosity.

Gournal

A "gournal" is simply a "guy's journal." Some men might not find it cool to journal, so "gournaling" might be a more appropriate word. When I was a young, lost man in my early twenties, a friend recommended to me that I start a journal. Initially, I thought this was silly and trivial, but I gave it a shot. What did I have to lose? I figured I could give up a little video game time or something that wasn't overproductive in my life.

My first entry in my first journal started with "So what's on my mind?" I stared at that question for a bit, and then suddenly, my hand couldn't stop writing. Thoughts and questions were gushing out of my mind, and I finally found a landing spot for these brain waves. Who am I? Why am I the way I am? What do I believe? What do I stand for? Who do I want to be when I grow up? Do I want to be married one day? Why or why not? Do I want to have kids? Why or why not? And the list kept going.

The best thing I could compare journaling to is having a raw, sincere conversation with a great friend who has great ears, great empathy, and truly cares about you. Man, we all need more people like that in our lives, don't we? If we had a person in our lives whom we could meet with weekly to have a great discussion, maybe there would be no need for a journal. I believe this is why many people find great value in seeing a therapist on a regular basis. Finally, there is someone who knows me, the real me; asks great questions; gets to the heart of the matter; doesn't let me off the hook with easy answers; and helps me become the person I'm capable of becoming. I've had my experiences with a therapist, and I can say that I greatly appreciated the time I spent with this therapist, which included weekly meetings for around six months. I gained clarity in understanding who I was and how I got there. I also built an understanding of what I didn't like about myself and came up with strategies on how to make changes. As I moved on from the therapy, I think I just let the journal become my new therapist, and I've kept the habit for almost thirty years now. My frequency for journaling isn't the same, but I am in the habit of sitting down in a quiet spot with my journal at least once per month.

Without the therapist, great friend, or journal, many thoughts can get stuck. Unfortunately, without proper vetting, we might be going down a path where our actions and behaviors are less than desirable, and we might not be becoming the person that we are capable of becoming. As discussed in the chapter "Who's the Best Teacher?" we would lose the opportunity to gain insight and wisdom without proper evaluated experience. I recommend engaging with all three (a therapist, a great friend, and a journal). The nice thing about the journal is that you don't have to put in much thought, planning, or money to get started. You can pick up a notebook today or start a Word document. Try doing what I did: "So what's on my mind?" I think you might be surprised that you have many unvetted thoughts that need a landing spot.

Think about this for a second: Do you get a lot of your best thoughts in the shower? I bet there's a high chance that you do. Do you know why so many of our best thoughts pop up in the shower? It's because we can't take our phones with us in the shower. It is one of the only times throughout the day that we are forced to "unplug." In our culture today, we can't stand in a line at Starbucks for two minutes without pulling out our phones to fill in the "dead air space." We're lost in the bathroom without our screens. I like consuming information as much as the next person, but I've come to recognize that consumption is a different muscle than creative thinking. When we unplug, it's amazing how creative our minds are capable of being. I heard that Albert Einstein wouldn't use any of his brain for memorizing anything that could be recorded. He wanted as much of his brain space available for creative thinking. We need constant (sometimes scheduled) quiet time to Grow Right; otherwise, we risk not being able to recognize that we are being told to think and feel the information we're being fed.

Life-Changing Events

Years ago, I had the privilege of reading *Lean In,* by Sheryl Sandberg. One of my big learnings from Sheryl is that many women "quit before they quit." In other words, instead of applying for a promotion or competing for advancements in their careers, many women take a back seat and let opportunities pass because they think about big upcoming changes, such as getting married and being mothers. My wife read the book and totally related to Sheryl's thoughts. She was in that boat herself, and she passed on several promotions in her law firm because she was thinking about motherhood on the horizon. Men don't have this same problem, and men will simply "go for it" because they are all about advancing their careers. However, men need to put some good thought into life-changing events, and men could learn from women on this subject. Not that men should "quit before they quit"; rather, we should think through how big life events are going to change our current world and think through what we can do to best prepare for it.

Since I was young, I always knew that I wanted to be married and have children. I started my own business in my early twenties and worked eighty-hour workweeks so I could get momentum going in my career. I was ambitious. As much as this was a good thing—so I thought—I dropped the ball in my early marriage years because I didn't "pivot." I thought I could keep working like this madman in pursuit of building a great life for my new bride and me, and I didn't think about nourishing the most important earthly relationship I'll ever have. I neglected my wife's needs to connect and have enough quality time together. I gave myself a pass at the time, because in my mind, I was grinding in business for her benefit, for our family's benefit. So I thought she would understand and encourage me to pursue my ambitions. I knew my intentions were good, but my ability to serve JoAnne was lacking.

Luckily, she was patient with me. I had some growing up and maturing to do. She prayed that good men and women would enter my life and help me prioritize my marriage and put as much effort into my marriage as I did my business. Thankfully, great men and women helped hold mirrors up for me to see myself as I truly was—as humbling as that could be. It was my responsibility to be the best husband for my wife, and I admitted that I could do a better job being much more attentive to JoAnne's needs.

As an example, every time I'd meet up with my mentor, Gary, for business conversations, he'd always spend more time making sure I was growing as a husband than he would making sure that I was winning in business. I finally came to the conclusion, thanks to Gary, that I would probably be successful in business because of my ambitious nature, but I could never lose sight of fulfilling "today's needs" for the most important person in my life. I'm also thankful for my men's group at church for holding me accountable to loving my wife the way Christ loved the church. When I finally had the courage to look at myself in the mirror as I truly was as a husband, I committed to my wife to be attentive, to make her feel like the most important person in my life, and to be the husband of the year (if there was such a thing). I set the expectations that I would work hard on my relationship with her and that she would see a change in my actions and behaviors. I started writing her notes every week, telling her how much I loved her and why I loved her. I put my money where my mouth was when I started shopping around for homes in Minnesota so my wife could be closer to her family. Leaving our good lives in beautiful Southern California for Minnesota was putting my priorities on the table for JoAnne. I wasn't officially crowned husband of the year, but I felt pretty good about my growth in this department.

There aren't many guarantees in life. I think it was Benjamin Franklin that said the only two guarantees in life are death and taxes. Let me add a third to Benji's list: change is a guarantee coming for us all. The only questions are will we be prepared for it, and will we successfully advance with change? Many people mistake Darwin's thoughts on survival of the fittest to be the survival of those who are strong or smart. The truth is, it's those who adapt and change to their environment that are considered "fit." Change is coming, and it's coming at a faster rate than previous generations. Don't let comfort zones prevent you from pursuing change. Get comfortable being uncomfortable.

Similar to my thoughts in the *Chicken Little* chapter, the key is choosing the influences proactively. Assemble the right people and procedures around you so that when life changes come, you don't have to make decisions in the moment. The decision has already been made in advance; now we just need to manage those decisions.

Here are a few questions that you can proactively ask yourself and start putting plans around:

- What are the most important characteristics that I want in a life partner? Why are those the most important things to me?
- What will change when I get married? Will my work look different? Will my lifestyle look different?
- What will my finances look like when I'm married? Will it be the same income I have now even though I'm going to increase my expenses? Will my household income grow?

- Will my income exceed my cost of living?
- Do I want to buy a home? Where will it be? How much will it cost? How can I prepare now for home ownership?
- Do I want children? Why or why not? How many do I want? What will look different? What kind of mother/father do I want to be? How involved will I be in my children's lives? Will my work look different? What do I want my work life to look like? Will I have help from family, friends, in-laws?

The habit of proactivity can aid our personal growth. Thinking proactively helps us solve problems that haven't occurred yet. I have a friend who proactively decided with his wife that any time an "extremely stressful situation" would arise, the two of them committed to traveling somewhere to talk and resolve—and not get their parents involved in the details. They would work through the difficulties of the situation as a couple.

There was an evening where the husband was in a precarious situation, and unfortunately, he was not faithful to his wife. He caved to the temptation of infidelity. He did not try to hide anything from his wife and came to her with complete remorse and regret. The proactive decision to "get away" was calling to both of them. I can't imagine how difficult that must have been for his wife to be alone with her cheating husband.

In their time together, he came to terms that he was not strong enough to handle the temptation, and he needed to grow closer to God. It became clear to both of them that God was missing in his life. When they went back home, they received biblical counseling, and he spent time with godly men from their church to discuss his infidelity and his lack of God in his life.

Fast-forward the clock: they both have tattoos of the date of the infidelity on their arms, as they have both grown closer to each other and God through that process. What a testimony they have! And what an example of what proactivity can look like if we're willing to have the courage to make tough decisions such as "getting away together" in the midst of the most difficult times in our lives. Don't wait until life-changing events happen to make these decisions.

Too many times I've seen people deal with life events as they happen, and they've found the pressure to be too much. It's very difficult to think straight and make good decisions when the pressure is boiling over. I've seen people divorce their spouses, leave their jobs or businesses, and leave their kids. Of course, these things were never in the plans. They never are. As the great theologian Mike Tyson once said, "Everyone has a plan until they get punched in the face." We can avoid a lot of pain if we are proactive and think through upcoming life changes before they are on our doorstep. We may still get "punched in the face," as Mike Tyson points out, but we've done our part to avoid the punch as best as we can by thinking through these events.

EGO

Depending on the survey, it seems like most people believe that God exists. The questions that I pose are these: Do you speak with God? Do you listen to God? Do you have a personal relationship with God?

From my observations, I think most people like to be independent, in control, and sprinkle a little "God" in their lives. We like to be the captains of our ships. But when tragedy happens, we don't mind taking second-in-command and let God fly the ship. The turbulence is too difficult for us, so we ask God for help. But when the turbulence is finished, we ask God to take a back seat and let us continue flying the plane to the destinations of our choosing. I challenge this train of thought because I don't think it's the healthiest approach. I don't believe that God wants to be a copilot for anyone. He *is* the pilot, and it's our job to align our will with his.

In my spiritual journey, I feel like I've gone the full circle.

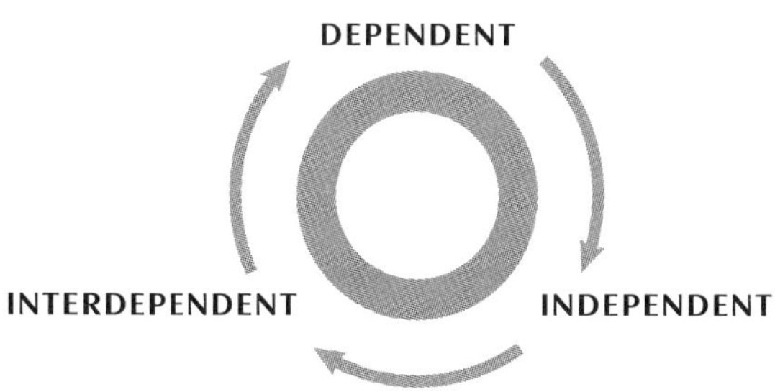

As a young man, I wanted to grow from being dependent to being independent. I wanted the freedom to spread my wings, make my own decisions, and be my own man. Then later, as an independent man, I wanted to collaborate and work with a team to become interdependent. I wanted to win with others; I decided I didn't want to live out my life as the lone ranger. I wanted my community and business associates to succeed as well. As an interdependent business owner and community member, I've come full circle to being back to dependent, but it's not dependency on others. It's dependency on my Maker. It has been said that when you get to the end of yourself, you get to the beginning of God.

I heard that the acronym for EGO is "Edging God Out." It's the pursuit of self and our passions and desires that tells God to take a back seat. I would encourage everyone to let God be the pilot of your life and allow yourself to take on the role of the passenger. I came across a great quote by Robert Rohr that helped me allow God to be the pilot of my life: "The opposite of faith is not doubt; the opposite of faith is control." I believe that God has a much better plan for our lives anyway, so why not let him drive our lives?

If you've ever been in Maui and driven the Hana Highway, you know how crazy this drive is. The Road to Hana, as it is called, is considered one of the most picturesque roads in the world, but it is also one of the most treacherous. It stretches for over sixty miles, has over fifty bridges, and many parts of this highway have 5 mph speed limits. It slows down to 5 mph because the road is literally a one-lane highway (at times) where vehicles need to stop and share the lane and take turns, allowing cars in the opposite direction the right of way.

On one of our vacations to Maui, JoAnne and I planned an overnight trip to Hana. It was beautiful driving out there, as expected. It was a six-hour drive, with beautiful weather and some breathtaking stops along the way. The next morning was stressful, to say the least. JoAnne woke up screaming with severe abdominal pain. We visited a local doctor in Hana. The doctor gave JoAnne a painkiller and sent us off to the hospital, where she could receive proper medical attention. The only problem was that we had to travel back on the Road to Hana to get the hospital. My rough math estimated that this drive would be four hours best-case scenario, and I was preparing myself for an extremely stressful drive.

The drive started with me gripping the steering wheel tightly and my heart pounding. I instinctively tapped into my aggressive Los Angeles driving, giving no one the right-of-way. About five minutes into the drive, it dawned on me that "I was flying the plane," and I needed to turn this over to God. As much as I felt like I was in control, it was clear that I needed him. I prayed with JoAnne, and I asked her to type a text for me to ask my friends back home to pray for us—to pray for JoAnne's health specifically and for a safe arrival driving to the hospital. Some prayer warriors in our corner were much needed. I'm relieved to report that we arrived at the Maui Memorial Medical Center around four hours later, and JoAnne successfully had her appendix removed.

The part of this story that is most interesting, in my opinion, was the peace that I had after that prayer. I stopped gripping the wheel, I slowed down to the appropriate speed limits, and I gave up complete control over the outcome of this stressful situation. Too many times I have focused on "My will be done." The Bible clearly states, "Thy will be done." This time I decided to let go and let God.

I've always appreciated John Wooden's perspective in coaching his players at UCLA when it came to dealing with their faith. He coached many boys from many different backgrounds. His stance was very simple: "Drink deeply from good books, especially the Bible." He encouraged his players to question and explore their faith. He believed that it was important that all players grow spiritually, get to know their Creator, and develop a personal relationship with God. Identify the "good books" and dive in and drink deep; don't just take a sip. Grow roots in your faith and drink for the rest of your life. I believe, and I think Coach Wooden would agree, that our physical, mental, and social lives will improve if we put more energy and focus on our spiritual lives. Or as Dr. Stephen Covey told a friend of mine, "You're a spiritual being having a human experience."

I recently heard of a "Ten-Step Cure" for anyone dealing with depression or sadness. Step 1: Find someone with greater needs than you and do something for that person. Take action. Step 2: Repeat step 1 nine more times. I don't think the author is trying to dismiss depression; rather, the goal is for the reader to shift the focus from "me" to "thee." I think that all major world religions buy into the paradigm of taking care of those less fortunate. I think when we are less concerned about ourselves, we will discover that we are called to love and take care of our brothers and sisters in need.

Our egos can take us out of serving others if we don't keep them in check. Our egos want to come through for self. Ego doesn't spend much time thinking about the needs of others. We need a big dose of humility in our lives. It has been said that people with humility don't think less of themselves; they just think of themselves less. Growing right, in my opinion, means growing closer to God and developing a relationship with him. A good friend of mine gave me some great marriage advice years ago. He said that a godly marriage is like a triangle, with the three points being God, your spouse, and you. He said that the closer you get to God, ultimately, the closer you'll get to your spouse. That advice has proven to be true in my life. Edging God Out results in a more distant relationship with my wife.

Let's check our egos and our self-interest at the door. I believe that a fulfilled life is one with a much higher purpose than just gaining personal pleasure. It is one that includes walking in harmony with your Maker.

What Glasses Are You Wearing?

As a door-to-door sales rep, my attitude was challenged every hour of every day. You never know who or what you'll see behind each new door. There was a day in particular that my tolerance for negative, rude customers was pretty low. I got to the point where I wasn't going to let people treat me poorly. I don't suggest that anyone does what I'm about to say here, as we all need to be professionals. This was one of those "aha" moments for me, and I want to share exactly how it happened.

I knocked on a door, and I could hear the angry, fast stomping coming closer and closer to the door. The angry stomp sound is always a sign that you're probably going to be greeted poorly.

"Hello, ma'am, how are you doing?"

"What do you want?" she said with a look of disgust on her face.

"I'm in your neighborhood today on behalf of—"

Then she practically screamed at me. "Stop what you're doing and just get out of here! You're not welcome here!"

With a low threshold for grumpy people, thinking my days as a door-to-door sales rep might be numbered soon, I responded, "Lady, why are you being so mean to me? It's not like you caught me making a mess in your front yard."

"I just found out my sister died!" she snapped.

In this split second, the glasses I was wearing were shattered.

My self-righteous, justice warrior glasses were completely broken, and my new glasses, coated in embarrassment and empathy, were now on my face.

"Oh, ma'am, I am so sorry. I shouldn't have said that, and I apologize. I will let you grieve. I'll be in your neighborhood for some time. Maybe I'll pop by next week."

Her body language changed. "No, I'm sorry. You're right. I never should have treated you the way I did. My personal issues shouldn't be taken out on other people. What are you selling?"

"No, ma'am, I'm in the wrong here. You're dealing with a heavy tragedy, and I'm sorry. I shouldn't be here. It's best that I leave you to yourself so that you can be with your family and grieve."

"No, I insist. I want to know what you're selling, and I'm the one in the wrong."

Our apologies went back and forth. It felt so awkward; I just wanted to leave and let her deal with her personal matters. However, she insisted I get my pitch out. As you can imagine, it was the quickest, shortest kind of pitch that was all summarized in under twenty seconds. Remarkably, she insisted on buying the promotion. I told her that she could sign up on a later date, and we did not have to conduct a transaction right now. Her insistence won, and I reluctantly sold her the promotion. This might have been the only reluctant sale I ever made. She was very kind and forgiving, and she wanted to make things right for a stranger that she had mistreated. I'll never forget this lady.

When I walked away from that door, I reflected on a very important lesson: whatever comes *out* of a person is probably what's going on *inside* of a person. Happy people don't hurt people. Only hurt people hurt people. What glasses do I choose to wear when I'm being mistreated? Before I met this lady, the glasses I was choosing to wear were coated in self. I am treated unjustly. I am treated poorly. It's all about me. Now that I had this encounter, I learned to be more aware and empathetic with others. Maybe the glasses I should wear from now on when I'm mistreated should be coated with love and empathy. There must be something wrong on the inside, and I should focus on them, not me. Those seem to be glasses that feel better—the glasses that are focused on adding value to others. I have learned that most of my trouble in life has been rooted in self. As Steve Wilburn says, "It's the unholy trinity of me, myself, and I." When I focus on my needs, my wants, and my desires, I have the potential to neglect how others are feeling and doing. It's not fulfilling to be focused on one's self. When I'm focused on others' needs and wants, I feel like I am a better version of myself.

My American journey started as a door-to-door sales rep in the summer of 1998. This was an exceptionally hot year in California; it wasn't the norm. It was so hot that planes in Phoenix had times when they couldn't fly because they couldn't get enough lift in the hot air. Also, a part of the road to Vegas was shut down because it was melting. And here I was, this foreigner to America, wearing a suit and going door to door. It felt like being in a sauna with a suit—hard to breathe, sweating buckets, and developing the most unusual tan anyone can imagine—dark brown hands and face and total white body everywhere else. I tried going to the beach on Sundays to even out the awkward tan; I was a little insecure.

I felt sorry for myself many days. The drive to the field was torture, as I knew what was in front of me as soon as I opened up that car door. I thought hell must be cooler than this.

Once again, my glasses were challenged on one of my drives. I listened to an AM radio station on the way to the field to get national news, international news, and sports highlights. At the time there was a war going on in the Middle East, and the reporter was doing a story from a hospital where a boy was recovering from a bomb blast. He was missing both his arms and legs, and his entire family (mother, father, and siblings) had perished. This young boy, I think he was nine, was expected to survive and would be living a very different life after this unthinkable event that took place.

Many times we can hear horrible stories like this one and just move past. And I get it; if we focus on listening to the horrors happening in this world all the time, we will be very depressed and probably crippled with inaction. We don't want to think about the pain and suffering that so many people endure. However, this time I stopped to really think about this boy. I tried to think of what life would be like if this happened to me. He was on my mind the entire day. As I was consumed with thoughts of him, I felt this overwhelming sense of embarrassment. Right before hearing this story, I was feeling sorry for myself because I had a long day ahead of me walking around the streets of Southern California in the heat, battling traffic and annoying drivers. I was thinking about some of the rude customers I would be encountering and how much these people would drive me crazy. I was slowly filling my mind with toxins that hadn't even happened, and I was creating a mindset of self-pity and low enthusiasm. But now my perspective had changed. Had I become self-absorbed and concerned only about myself?

I have learned that gratitude and envy cannot coexist in the same heart. They cannot be roommates. One will be present, and the other will be absent. It is up to me to decide which one will be present. I can wear the envy glasses, or I can wear the gratitude glasses. Each is the nemesis of the other.

When I think about the lady who was dealing with her sister passing away, I was focused on myself, and envy was present because most of my friends had easier jobs where they didn't have to deal with the challenges that I was dealing with. When I think about the young boy in the Middle East, I was once again focused on myself and the ever-present envy of others not having to put up with walking around the desert with a suit on. I have learned that if gratitude is not present, if those glasses are unintentionally missing, then envy creeps in to reside in my heart. I didn't ask envy to come in. There wasn't an open invitation. It just slithered in silently.

In my daily prayer life, I set aside some of that time to focus on gratitude. I should really take nothing for granted. Every good thing happening in my life is a gift. I try to fill myself with gratitude—many times I'll focus on the big things I'm thankful for such as living in America or being with my beautiful, healthy family. Other times I'll focus on some of the smaller things, such as the convenience of Starbucks by my house or that my car runs fine today or that I still have some hair growing on my head. The discipline of daily gratitude is my weapon against the unwanted enemy of envy residing in my mindset. Wear the glasses of gratitude and we'll find ourselves growing right, absent of the silent joy killer that envy produces.

Pay Now, Play Later

I walked past a used car dealership recently that had a poster on their window of a happy customer driving a convertible. Under the beautiful picture was the slogan, "Play Now, Pay Later." That might be a big problem in our culture, and it certainly concerns many of us about our national "pay later" economy and our national debt. I once heard Americans described this way: we spend money we don't have to buy things that we don't need to impress others we don't even like in the first place. We're probably all a little guilty of this to a certain degree.

As a child, I remember watching TV commercials for vehicles, and they always had price tags such as $19,999. I'd ask my dad why they played tricks like that with people and didn't advertise the cars at $20,000. Today, it's difficult to find a car commercial where they disclose the full price of the vehicle. Instead, they advertise the monthly payment. We've been sucked into a Play Now, Pay Later economy.

It's counterculture to avoid the monthly recurring payments lifestyle. It's difficult to put off the immediate impulse, save cash, and only buy things when you can afford them. This is what delaying gratification is all about. Delayed gratification is the act of resisting temptation for an immediate benefit in the hope of acquiring a much more important benefit in the future. Of course, we all want to drive that convertible like the guy in the picture, but suppressing that desire and having the self-control is what Pay Now, Play Later is all about.

If you google "Dr. Edward Banfield, Harvard, long-term perspective," you'll see some interesting observations that Dr. Banfield and his team discovered. Dr. Banfield of Harvard University, after more than fifty years of research, concluded that "long-term perspective" is the most accurate single predictor of upward social and economic mobility in America. Long-term perspective turns out to be more important than family background, education, race, intelligence, connections, or virtually any other single factor in determining your success in life and at work. Powerful stuff!

Here's how I see it: There are two different life strategies; we have two options as we go through life:

1. Play now and pay later.
2. Pay now and play later.

In both scenarios, the good news is that we get to play. In both scenarios the bad news is that we must pay. But here's the kicker: whatever it is that you choose, understand that the latter of the two will be exponential. In other words, if you choose to play now and pay later (for example, purchasing a vehicle that you can't afford), you'll be paying exponentially. You'll be paying interest and a greater price. But if you choose to pay now and play later, then you'll be playing exponentially. You'll be able to play on a grander scale than you thought and potentially for longer.

The life option of "pay now and play later" was one of the toughest decisions for me to buy into as a young man in my early twenties but one that has made a huge difference in my life. I had difficulty investing so much effort on the front end of my new career as a salesperson and entrepreneur. I was overworked and underpaid, and when I compared my life with those of my friends, it seemed like a hard pill to swallow. I wanted to work less and have more time to enjoy life, such as playing recreational sports, spending more time with friends and family, traveling, and so on. However, I made the choice to front-load my career. I came to the conclusion that it was okay to be overworked and underpaid because that seemed to be the formula for every successful athlete, business owner, rock star, you name it, who was living the life of eventually being underworked and overpaid. If you think about it, being overworked and underpaid in the beginning of one's career is the price tag for not having to be so overworked in your older years. I figured what was really important in the long run is to have the time and resources when I was older to be with my future wife, my future children, and maybe become involved in philanthropy or something really meaningful as I grew older.

As mentioned earlier, I eventually had to hold a mirror up as a husband and come to terms that I needed to invest more into my relationship with JoAnne. And I did just that. Just like attending business seminars, I invested my time and energy in marriage seminars and nourished the most important relationship in this earthly life. My needed improvement for being a present husband wasn't caused by a Pay Now, Play Later mentality. I just needed to grow up and be relentless about being a great husband for the long-term benefit of my marriage.

I'm hoping that every reader buys into the life strategy of Pay Now, Play Later because it might be one of the most important decisions we'll make. Paying on the front end doesn't have to be gruesome or unappealing. Working hard can be fun, and you'll make some great new like-minded, long-term friends, which will be very rewarding. I think if we can make "the pay" a ton of fun, maybe even gamify paying, it'll be easier to buy into this strategy, and I highly doubt you'll regret buying into it.

I had a discussion years ago with a friend who bought into the opposite strategy. He believed that life is too short, and he wanted to play now. He said to me, "Hepp, what if you get hit by a bus? You missed out on all of that playtime because you were so focused on the pay."

I said, "You know, you might be right, and I certainly need to make sure that I'm working on making the pay a little more playful. But I want you to think about this: What if you're *not* hit by a bus?" There was a long pause after that. "What would life look like if you dedicated your life to playing and you weren't hit by a bus?"

I'll end this chapter with the following quote by an anonymous author, which I believe is the masterful way of employing the Pay Now, Play Later mindset:

> "The master in the art of living makes little distinction between his work and his play, his labor and his leisure, his mind and his body, his education and his recreation, his love and his religion. He hardly knows which is which. He simply pursues his vision of excellence at whatever he does, leaving others to decide whether he is working or playing. To him he is always doing both."

Final Thoughts

I have heard that the enemy of great is not poor. The enemy of great is good. When things are good, we tend to be content, and we aren't striving for improvement. I hear many people talking about the "history of the world" and its cycle, which goes something like this:

- Bad times create strong people.
- Strong people create good times.
- Good times create weak people.
- Weak people create bad times.

I tell my children that we are in the "good times" part of the cycle. This doesn't mean that we need to accept the outcome that's identified in this cycle. To think that your destiny is to be weak is upsetting. I challenge them and I'll challenge you: there is one remedy to live during good times and still come out of it a strong person. That remedy is to be hungry. Be hungry for growth, be hungry to level up, and don't be content with the status quo. Grow! Grow Right! Grow Right Now!

Here's a riddle I tell my kids: "Five birds are on a wire. Three of them decide to fly south for the winter. How many birds are left on the wire?"

Many think the answer is two. But the answer is five. Five birds remain on the wire. Deciding isn't enough. Thinking isn't enough. Action is at the center of Grow Right. It's the art of doing. These three birds have to decide, *and then* they must act.

My hope is that you, whether you are one of my three children or you are a stranger whom I've never met, are inspired to level up and apply some of these Grow Right principles to your life. David Goggins recently said, "You are in danger of living life so comfortable that you will never know your full potential." Don't let your good life stop you from growing into the best version of you. It's a matter of picking your battles and priorities and then the art of willful execution.

GROW. GROW RIGHT. GROW RIGHT NOW. is written for those not only striving for personal growth but those who are also seeking to develop in character—growing right. The author devoted fourteen years to writing this book for his children and has now shared these engaging stories and timeless wisdom with the world. Be prepared to laugh, cry, and be challenged by many truths that will prompt a reflective look in the mirror and inspire growth—right now.

"Read this feel-good book—
then get out there and make a difference!"

Ken Blanchard, coauthor of *The One Minute Manager®* and *Simple Truths of Leadership*

JAIME HEPP is a husband, father, and businessman in Orange County, California. He has spent the past three decades developing salespeople, business owners, and entrepreneurs throughout the United States and Canada. As the world has changed, Jaime has stayed true to his principles while evolving both personally and professionally to meet the demands of the times. When not leading his business, Jaime has been active in his community serving as a board member of the local Boys & Girls Club and coaching a variety of youth sports. In his leisure time, Jaime loves spending time with his wife and three children.

JAIMEHEPP.COM

amplify
an imprint of Amplify Publishing Group

ISBN 979-8-89138-308-1
US $16.00
CAN $26.00
51600
9 798891 383081